# THEOLOGICAL AND LITURGICAL UNDERSTANDING OF GESTURES, VENERATION AND SYMBOLISM

## With Regard to the Altar and Their Implications for Today

Rev. Alexander Mariadass, Ph.D.

**W. R. PARKS**
www.WRParks.com

Copyright © 2020 by Alexander Mariadass

ISBN: **978-0-88493-063-1**

Published by William R. Parks  www.wrparks.com

Hershey, PA, 17033 USA

DEDICATED

TO

MY BELOVED PARENTS

MARIADASS ANTHONY MUTHU

ALPHONSE CRUZ MANICKAM DEVASAGAYAM

# ACKNOWLEDGEMENT

"Rejoice in the Lord always. I will say it again: Rejoice!" (Phil 4, 4)

My heart is filled with gratitude to Almighty God who has blessed me with His unconditional providence during the years of my study in Rome, especially during this work. May His name be glorified.

With sentiments of profound gratitude, I would like to acknowledge the support of many people who tirelessly contributed toward ensure the completion of this task. First and foremost, I sincerely thank my moderator, His Excellency Professor Manel Nin OSB. In spite of his busy life in the university and new responsibility as a bishop, he was there in my moments of need and guided with valuable suggestions, scholarly words of wisdom and encouragement.

Likewise, I am also grateful to all my professors at *Pontificio Ateneo Sant' Anselmo* who have brought me to a better understanding of the Sacred Liturgy. I express my deep sentiments of gratitude to my diocese of Coimbatore, especially to my bishop Most Rev. Thomas Aquinas for providing me this great opportunity to do the licentiate in Liturgy.

Furthermore, my humble gratitude also goes to the Congregation for the Evangelization of Peoples for granting me a scholarship and accommodation. I specially thank the Rector and the staff of *Pontificio Collegio S. Pietro Apostolo* and the fellow student priests for their care and support. I gratefully remember my family members and friends who stood by me with their loving support, encouragement and prayers.

Lastly but not least, together with Fr. William Prabu and Fr. Antony Jesuraj, Mrs. Christina Paino, form Hauppauge, New York, who, with their love and support, spent time to do the proofreading and making necessary corrections and suggestions, I would like to thank all those who supported me in during my stay in Italy.

# ABBREVIATIONS

The following are the abbreviations cited in this work.

| | | |
|---|---|---|
| AAS | - | *Acta Apostolica Sedis* |
| Ca. | - | Circa |
| Can. | - | Canon |
| ff. | - | following |
| GeV | - | *Gelesianum Vetus* |
| GIRM | - | General Instruction of the Roman Missal |
| ICEI | - | International Committee on English in the Liturgy |
| No. | - | Number |
| OT | - | Old Testament |
| PG | - | *Patrologia Greca* |
| PL | - | *Patrologia Latina* |
| RM | - | Roman Missal |
| SC | - | *Sacrosanctum Concilium* |
| U.S. | - | United States |

The following abbreviations are used for the books of the Bible in this work:

**Old Testament**

| | | |
|---|---|---|
| Gen | - | Genesis |
| Ex | - | Exodus |
| Lev | - | Leviticus |
| Deut | - | Deuteronomy |
| Jos | - | Joshua |
| Jud | - | Judges |
| 1 Sam | - | 1 Samuel |
| 1 Kgs | - | 1 Kings |
| Ps | - | Psalm |
| Eze | - | Ezekiel |
| Hos | - | Hosea |
| 1 Mac | - | 1 Maccabeus |

**New Testament**

| | | |
|---|---|---|
| Mt | - | Matthew |
| Mk | - | Mark |
| Lk | - | Luke |
| Jn | - | John |
| Rom | - | Romans |
| 1 Cor | - | 1 Corinthians |
| 2 Cor | - | 2 Corinthians |
| Eph | - | Ephesians |
| Col | - | Colossians |
| 1 Thes | - | 1 Thessalonians |
| Heb | - | Hebrews |
| 1Pet | - | 1 Peter |
| Rev | - | Revelation |

## TABLE OF CONTENTS

ACKNOWLEDGEMENT ................................................................................................ IV

ABBREVIATIONS ......................................................................................................... V

GENERAL INTRODUCTION ........................................................................................ 1

**CHAPTER ONE: BIBLICAL AND HISTORICAL EVOLUTION OF THE IDEA OF THE ALTAR** ................................................................................................................ 5

    1.1. BIBLICAL EVOLUTION OF THE IDEA OF THE ALTAR ................................... 5

        1.1.1. ETYMOLOGY OF THE TERM ALTAR ....................................................... 5

        1.1.2. OLD TESTAMENT VIEW OF THE ALTAR ................................................ 7

        1.1.3. NEW TESTAMENT VIEW OF THE ALTAR ............................................... 9

    1.2. HISTORICAL EVOLUTION OF THE IDEA OF THE ALTAR ............................ 10

        1.2.1. ALTARS IN PAGAN RELIGIONS ............................................................. 10

        1.2.2. HISTORY OF THE CHRISTIAN ALTAR ................................................... 12

        1.2.3. THE ALTAR IN THE PATRISTIC WRITINGS .......................................... 16

        1.2.4. THE ALTAR IN CONCILIAR AND OTHER CHURCH DOCUMENTS ....... 19

    1.3. CENTRALITY OF THE ALTAR IN THE LITURGY ............................................ 22

        1.3.1. TABERNACLE AND THE ALTAR ............................................................ 22

        1.3.2. ORIENTATION AND THE ALTAR ........................................................... 25

        1.3.3. RELICS AND THE ALTAR ....................................................................... 28

    CONCLUSION TO THE FIRST CHAPTER .................................................................. 33

**CHAPTER TWO: UNDERSTANDING GESTURES, VENERATION AND SYMBOLISM WITH REGARD TO THE ALTAR** ........................................................ 36

    2.1. GESTURES AND VENERATION CENTERED AROUND THE ALTAR ............ 36

        2.1.1. INCENSING THE ALTAR ......................................................................... 38

        2.1.2. KISSING THE ALTAR .............................................................................. 43

- 2.1.3. BOWING AND GENUFLECTING BEFORE THE ALTAR ............ 46
- 2.1.4. ADORNMENT OF THE ALTAR .......................................... 49
  - 2.1.4.1. ALTAR CLOTHS ............................................. 51
  - 2.1.4.2. ALTAR CROSS ............................................... 54
  - 2.1.4.3. ALTAR CANDLES ........................................... 58
  - 2.1.4.4. ALTAR FLOWERS .......................................... 62
- 2.2. SYMBOLISM OF THE ALTAR .................................................. 66
  - 2.2.1. THE SYMBOL OF COVENANT AND COMMUNION ............... 67
  - 2.2.2. THE SYMBOL OF TABLE ............................................... 72
  - 2.2.3. THE SYMBOL OF CHRIST .............................................. 75
- CONCLUSION TO THE SECOND CHAPTER ......................................... 78

# CHAPTER THREE: THEOLOGICAL AND LITURGICAL UNDERSTANDING AND THEIR IMPLICATIONS .......... 80

- 3.1. THEOLOGICAL AND LITURGICAL UNDERSTANDING ................ 80
  - 3.1.1. CHRISTOCENTRIC UNDERSTANDING ............................. 80
  - 3.1.2. ECCLESIOLOGICAL UNDERSTANDING ............................ 86
  - 3.1.3. SACRIFICIAL UNDERSTANDING ..................................... 90
- 3.2. IMPLICATIONS FOR TODAY ................................................... 94
  - 3.2.1. LITURGICAL IMPLICATIONS ......................................... 94
  - 3.2.2. PASTORAL IMPLICATIONS ............................................ 97
  - 3.2.3. SOME GUIDELINES AND PROPOSALS FOR TODAY ............ 101
- CONCLUSION TO THE THIRD CHAPTER ........................................... 105
- GENERAL CONCLUSION ................................................................ 107
- **BIBLIOGRAPHY** ........................................................................ 109

# GENERAL INTRODUCTION

In every church, the altar is centrally located. From the earliest days of the Catholic Church, the altar was an object of great veneration, the most sacred place in the church. At the beginning of Mass, the very first act of veneration is paid to the altar. The liturgy is initiated by God on humankind's behalf. In the liturgy, the altar is the most important element towards which all actions are oriented.

It is at the altar where there is a meeting of God and man and a wonderful exchange takes place between God and man. In this meeting and wonderful exchange, gestures and veneration play important roles. Liturgy is the action of God through the Church. In the action of God, man surrenders himself with the help of gestures, veneration and symbols.

Moreover, the altar is understood only by the actions that take place around it. Therefore, if one needs to know the real meaning and value of the altar, he or she has to observe what takes place at the altar and what are the objects placed around it. This is where the importance of studying gestures, veneration and symbolism with regard to altar become necessary. The reverence shown to the altar flows from the typology of the altar, as Christ, throne of God, Symbol of Covenant, Lord's table, etc. In his or her relationship to the altar, every Christian must remember that the altar is Christ and that he or she is a spiritual altar.

## EXPLORATION OF THE THEME

The sacrifice of Christ is the focal point of salvation history. Jesus wanted to perpetuate and continue the sacrifice on the cross by the breaking of the bread. This Eucharistic celebration is celebrated on the altar. By the Sacrifice offered on it, the altar becomes the place of most importance. The fifth preface of the Easter season narrates that Christ is the Priest, the Victim and the altar. As the altar plays an important role in the liturgy and many of the liturgical ceremonies are on and around altar, I would like to explore the deeper understanding of the gestures, veneration and symbols with regard to the altar. The idea came to me from the explanation of Prof. Manel Nin when he was teaching about the ordination of the priests in the Byzantine rite. He explained that when the priest is ordained the Bishop touches the altar with one hand and imposes the other hand on the priest, signifying that the bishop communicates the sanctity from the altar. And in the study of the history of *Missale Romanum*, Prof. Cassian Folsom also explained the importance of the altar and the gestures related to the altar such as touching, kissing and genuflecting. These actions around the altar triggered me to ponder some of the important gestures, veneration and symbolism with regard to the altar. After a serious study, I thought of developing the theme on the theological and liturgical understanding of gestures, veneration and symbolism with regard to the altar and their implications for today. I thought it would be a great contribution to the science of liturgy. Moreover, personally I feel it is very important for each one of us to understand the deeper meaning of the gestures, veneration and symbolism with regard to the altar and perform them meaningfully.

## THE OBJECTIVES OF THE WORK

1. It is a genuine effort to explore the deeper meaning of the altar and gestures, veneration and symbolism which are centred around the altar.
2. To bring to light the liturgical and theological understanding of the gestures, veneration and symbolism with regard to the altar.
3. Inviting all to realize that gestures and veneration are not only customs or rituals, but they have strong theological significances which can be expressed by non-verbal actions.
4. To establish the importance of the value and significance of the gestures, veneration and symbolism with regard to the altar and to suggest some practical guidelines for today with regard to the altar.

## SCOPE AND SIGNIFICANCE OF THIS WORK

The scope of this research is to open up and to rediscover the inner richness of the non-verbal elements of prayer around the altar and the symbolism of it in the Roman rite. I firmly believe that this study profoundly emphasizes the significance within the scope of the gestures, veneration and symbolism with regard to the altar. The practical implications proposed are intended to help the celebrant to realize what he does and the community to understand the non-verbal elements in the liturgy around the altar. Hence this work would contribute to the theological and liturgical understanding of gestures, veneration and symbolism with regard to the altar and enable the celebrant and the participants to know that in the liturgy every element has a rich meaning and strong biblical and historical background. Therefore I am certainly sure that this work would contribute to towards the veneration and reverence of the altar that every celebrant and the participants should have.

## THE METHOD USED TO DEVELOP THIS WORK

I have divided the entire work into three chapters. The first chapter discusses the biblical and historical evolution of the idea of the altar. In order to arrive at the understanding of the altar proper, I am trying to explain the evolution of the idea of the altar in Biblical sources and historical evidences. In second chapter, I will discuss the understanding of gestures, veneration and symbolism with regard to altar. In discussing the veneration, the altar decoration is also considered to be an expression of a form of veneration of the altar. Though there are many symbolisms that can be found for the altar, I will discuss only three important symbolisms of altar in this work and try to explore them in detail. In the third chapter, I would like to take into consideration the theological and liturgical understanding of gestures, symbolism and veneration with regard to the altar. In the final chapter, the implications for today, is discussed with liturgical and pastoral views and some proposals for better understanding and implementing of these gestures, veneration and symbolisms are given.

## LIMITATIONS OF THE WORK

As far as limitations are concerned, I will discuss only three elements with regard to the altar: Gestures, Veneration and Symbolism. These discussions will be limited to the Roman rite. With regard to the Roman rite, I have found sufficient materials and references in the form of biblical, liturgical, and magisterial works, dictionaries, encyclopaedias, books, and articles. Since I have decided to discover the theological and liturgical understanding of gestures, veneration and symbolism with regard to the altar in the Roman rite and their implications for today, I have a greater responsibility to do justice to my work honestly.

# CHAPTER ONE
# BIBLICAL AND HISTORICAL EVOLUTION OF THE IDEA OF THE ALTAR

The Christian Altar did not appear suddenly. It was long in the making. Before the dawn of history, man made the Altar. As the truth about God and his relation to God broke upon his consciousness, man hastened to build the Altar and from that moment until the end of time the history of mankind will be the history of the Altar[1]. In this chapter, I would like to deal with the evolution of the idea of the Altar from the Biblical and Historical perspective. The main theme of this study is to deepen our understanding of the gestures, veneration and symbolism with regard to the Altar and their implications for today. For this purpose, one should know what is the Altar and why it is given such importance and veneration. For this, the Biblical and Historical aspects will be of help.

## 1.1. BIBLICAL EVOLUTION OF THE IDEA OF THE ALTAR

In the Bible, there are many forms of worship. Beginning with the book of Genesis until the book of Revelation, one can see many evidences of the existence of the Altar in the encounter between God and man. However, the importance of the Altar in worship grew gradually and when worship was centralized in the temple, the Altar became the centre of the sacrifice. Under this topic, the etymology of the word 'Altar' is dealt with and I limit myself to the essential and overall view of the evolution of the idea of the Altar in the books of the Bible.

### 1.1.1. ETYMOLOGY OF THE TERM ALTAR

The Altar is the central point of the relationship between God and Man. To see the evolution of the Altar, one should first see the Biblical understanding of the term Altar. The most common Hebrew word for Altar in the Old Testament is מִזְבֵּחַ (*mizbeah*) from the root *zbh*, meaning 'to slaughter'. Although *mizbeah* probably meant at first 'that upon which the victim was slaughtered', later the victim was slaughtered at a

---

[1] M. J. BEHEN, «The Christian Altar», in *Worship* 26 (1952) 422-428, 422.

distance from the Altar and then placed upon it[2]. The word '*mizbeah*' resembles four other words meaning 'removes evil decrees', 'sustains', 'endears' and 'atones'. C. Edsman tries to explain the word by using it as an acronym stating that the four consonants of *mizbeah* are sometimes also interpreted as the initial letters of the four words meaning 'forgiveness', 'justification', 'blessing', 'life'[3].

The Greek equivalent for *mizbeah* is θυσιαστήριον which means an 'Altar' connected to sacrifice. The early Church was referring to the Eucharist as θυσια which means 'sacrifice'. The table at which it was celebrated was θυσιαστήριον, which means 'place of sacrifice', the term for the Altar first used in the Septuagint. The commonly used term among the Christians was τράπεζα which means 'table'[4]. In the Greek-speaking East in the present day the usual expression for Altar is Ἁγία or Ἱερά τράπεζα (the holy or sacred table)[5]. The ancient meaning has been further verified by the corresponding Classical Greek term βωμός which means 'raised platform, stand, base, Altar with a base or the foundation of the sacrifice'. Further Edsman affirms that we can find the term βωμός used throughout the Bible to designate the altars of the pagan gods[6].

The Latin origin of the term Altar is *Altare*. Many explanations are given as to the etymology of *Altare* and *ara* by grammarians and philologists. Nicholas, quoting Festus, the Roman grammarian, gives three classifications:

> a) *Altare* is from *adolescere*, 'to burn or to be kindled', because on it the flames rose up.
> b) *Altare* is from *adolere*, 'to burn or consume by fire', because on the Altar the offering was burnt up or consumed.
> c) *Altare* is from *altus*, *altitudo*, because the *Altaría* consecrated to the higher deities show a construction rising up from the earth, being built up high[7].

The Christians differentiated their Altars from pagan ones by using the terms *Altare* and *mensa* instead of *ara*, and by referring to their Altar in the singular, reserving

---

[2] P. J. KEARNEY, «Altar in the Bible», in *New Catholic Encyclopedia Vol I*, ed. W. J. Mc Donald, McGraw-Hill Book Company, New York 1967, 344-346, 344.
[3] C. EDSMAN, «Altar», in *The Encyclopedia of Religion Vol I*, ed. E. Mircea, Macmillan Publishing Company, New York 1987, 222-226, 225.
[4] C. EDSMAN, «Altar», 226.
[5] S. SALAVILLE, *An Introduction to the Study of Eastern Liturgies*, Sands & Co, London 1938, 133.
[6] C. EDSMAN, «Altar», 225.
[7] M. NICHOLAS, *Altars according to the Code of Canon Law*, The Catholic University of America, Washington 1927, 11-12.

the plural *altaria* for pagan places of sacrifice[8]. The English word *Altar*, meaning 'a raised structure of which sacrifices are offered to a deity', derives from Latin *Altare* and may be related to *altus*[9]. In older English, usage of the word Altar is often meant God's board, and this expression is especially used when reference is made to Holy Communion[10].

## 1.1.2. OLD TESTAMENT VIEW OF THE ALTAR

There are three types of Altar in the Old Testament: the Altar of earth (Ex 20, 21–23), the Altar of stones (Deut 27, 2-8), and the Altar of wood covered with bronze and with horns at each of the four corners[11]. Nicholas beautifully gives the chronological development of Altar in the Bible as follows:

> The erection of an Altar is first mentioned in Holy Scripture when Noah built an Altar after the safe delivery from the ark (Gen 8, 20). Thereafter mention is made of Altars erected by Abraham (Gen 12, 7-8; 22, 9), Isaac (Gen 26, 25), Jacob (Gen 33, 20; 35, 7), and Moses (Ex 17, 15). These simple structures used as Altars were usually erected in places where God had manifested His goodness or a special favor or blessing in some particular manner. About the material or form of the Altars of the patriarchs, we can see the example of Jacob on the morning after his mysterious dream in setting up a stone and anointing it (Gen 28, 16-19) and from the later prescription of the Mosaic Law (Ex 20, 24-25) that they were elevations made from earth or unhewn stones[12].

The Altars in the Old Testament can be lay Altars and priestly Altars from the aspect of the ministers and its functions. The earliest practice presupposes the use of Altars in a worship attended by no special priesthood. Instead the priestly Altars were at the door of the tabernacle or tent of the meeting where no lay person is allowed to sacrifice except the priests and there was an incense Altar also inside the sacred tent[13].

Behen says that if the Old Testament was a religion of Altar and sacrifice, it was only that men might be prepared for the Altar and sacrifice of the New Testament.

---

[8] C. EDSMAN, «Altar», 225.
[9] C. EDSMAN, «Altar», 222.
[10] T. BRIDGET, *A History of the Holy Eucharist in Great Britain*, C. Kegan Paul & Co, London 1881, 191.
[11] P. HEGER, *The Three Biblical Altars*, Werner Hildebrand, Berlin 1999, 14-15.
[12] M. NICHOLAS, *Altars according to the Code of Canon Law*, 2.
[13] H. M. WIENER, «Altar», in *The International Standard Bible Encyclopedia Vol I*, ed. G. F. Bromiley, William B. Eerdmans Publishing Company, Michigan 1979, 100-104, 100-101.

All the Altars of Israel, from the primitive Altar of earth erected by Moses at the foot of Mount Sinai to the richly ornamented Altar in the temple at Jerusalem, all were figures of the present time, the New Covenant of God with His people. We can learn reverence for the Altar as we contemplate the pious Jew before his Altar. For him the Altar, though built by human hands, was the throne of God, and merely to touch it, was to be made holy (Ex 29, 37). The gift placed on the Altar was sanctified merely by contact with the Altar[14].

When we analyse the material of the Altar, we find that raw, unpolished stones were used as Altars and there were also Altars constructed either of mud or of brick. The ancient laws of Exodus 20, 24-26 permitted either material, but there is no clear indication as to which was more generally used. There is always the desire to separate the divine from the human which is probably the origin of the law against steps leading up to the Altar (Ex 20, 26). The carved horns were considered as the most sacred parts of the Altar (Ex 29, 12)[15].

Above all, the Altar was a symbol of God's presence. Thus Abraham and Jacob built Altars to commemorate a theophany[16] (Gen 13, 18; 35, 7), as did Gideon, even giving a theophoric[17] name to his Altar: 'Yahweh-Peace' (Jud 6, 24). At the Altar, communion was achieved with God, as the offerings were removed from the human sphere to the divine, and blessings were received from God in return (Ex 20, 24). The sprinkling of blood on the worshipers and the Altar brought the people into communion with God Himself (Ex 24, 6). The Altar was a symbol of communion and blessing and the horns of the Altar was a special sign of God's protective presence[18].

There is also mention of the incense Altar. Like the desert Altar of holocausts, it is a portable Altar, built of wood and carried with poles. It is, however, also plated with gold, and so is known as 'the golden Altar'. The existence of this Altar just outside the Holy of Holies in Solomon's Temple is well documented in Isaiah 6, 6. Under the

---

[14] M. J. BEHEN, «The Christian Altar», 423.
[15] P. J. KEARNEY, «Altar in the Bible», 344-345.
[16] A visible manifestation of God to humankind.
[17] Bearing the name of God
[18] P. J. KEARNEY, «Altar in the Bible», 345.

Maccabees an incense Altar was reinstalled (1Mac 4, 49), although doubtful that it was the same one at which Zachary offered incense (Lk 1, 8-10)[19].

In the description of the Altar in the Old Testament, one can see there are different kinds of Altars, according to the usage, like, the Altar of holocausts and the Altar of incense, according to the material used, like, stone Altars, mud brick Altars, and wooden, bronze or golden Altars and the idea of the Altar is to emphasize the presence of God and to thank God for the gifts received. It is a symbol of communion and the protective power of God.

### 1.1.3. NEW TESTAMENT VIEW OF THE ALTAR

The Altar has a completely different meaning in the New Testament. The most important Altar of all that supersedes all other Altars is the cross on which Jesus sacrificed himself. Jesus' words reflect the Old Testament symbolism of the Altar as the sign of God's presence. He speaks about the sacredness of the Altar. It is the Altar that designates a gift as victim (Mt 23, 19), that signifies its offering to God and its acceptance by Him[20].

Christ, our Lord and Redeemer, had celebrated the first Eucharistic sacrifice upon a table, and it was surely also a table which the Apostles in imitation of Him used on their missionary journeys. Thus St. Paul in his first epistle to the Corinthians (1Cor 10, 21) speaks expressly of a τραπέζης κυρίου, *mensa Domini*, 'table of the Lord'. The Altar, consequently, is rather an outgrowth of Catholic dogma concerning the Holy Eucharist as the non-bloody sacrifice of the New Law and the sacrament wherein the souls of men are replenished with the Body and Blood of Christ, the Saviour[21].

The image of the rock is closely connected to Christ in the New Testament and St. Paul identifies this rock as Christ (1Cor 10, 4). Ferraro explaining the Biblical background concludes that as Jesus is also its unique temple, priest and victim, He himself is the unique Altar of the New Law (Heb 13, 10)[22]. Paul contrasted the Christian service with the pagan sacrificial meal by stating that we cannot partake of the Lord's

---

[19] P. J. KEARNEY, «Altar in the Bible», 346.
[20] J. B. O'CONNELL, *Church Building and Furnishing*, Burns & Oates, London 1955, 133.
[21] M. NICHOLAS, *Altars according to the Code of Canon Law*, 2-3.
[22] G. FERRARO, *Cristo è l'Altare: Liturgia di dedicazione della chiesa e dell'Altare*, Edizioni OCD, Roma 2004, 210-214.

table and the devil's table at the same time (1Cor 10, 21). He thus distinguished between pagan sacrificial altars and the table at which Christ celebrated the Last Supper[23]. There are some places in the books of Hebrews and Revelation where an Altar is mentioned, but that Altar is in heaven, not on earth (Heb 7, 13; 13, 10 and Rev 6, 9; 8, 3-5; 11, 1). The Altar here on earth is not the final Altar. There is still another Altar, and that is the glorious fulfilment of the Christian Altar[24]. In the New Testament, there is a new approach to the Altar. The Altar is Christ centred and it is more spiritual than material.

## 1.2. HISTORICAL EVOLUTION OF THE IDEA OF THE ALTAR

Under this topic, I am going to discuss the historical viewpoint of the Altar in four aspects. In history, we see almost all religions used some means to worship God and the role of the Altar in the worship is noteworthy. The Altar was a symbol of the unseen presence of the gods and was therefore considered a sacred spot. Used as a table: it invited the god to partake of the offering; used as a throne it bade the God to take his place. The shape of the hearth reflected the transformation of the sacrifice, through fire, into matter appropriate for the spiritual world[25].

### 1.2.1. ALTARS IN PAGAN RELIGIONS

For every religion in which sacrifices and offerings comprise the most solemn ritual for establishing and repairing the relationship between God and the worshiper, the Altar upon which the sacrifice is made stands in a central position. It is in one sense the focal point of this relationship, the concrete structure at the heart of the act of communication between humanity and God[26]. Each religion has a form of worship and mostly all of them have a type of sacrifice involving the Altar. In this topic, I would like to describe the usage of Altar in some of the ancient and famous religions, which use the Altar in their worship.

The Altar in Greek religions is a raised place, usually an artificial structure, which is used for the purpose of making offerings to a god or gods. It is different from

---

[23] C. EDSMAN, «Altar», 225.
[24] M. J. BEHEN, «The Christian Altar», 427.
[25] C. EDSMAN, «Altar», 222-223.
[26] T. HIEBERT, «Altars of Stone and Bronze: Two Biblical Views of Technology», in *Mission Studies 15* (1998/2) 75-84, 76.

altars of other religions. It is like a table of banquet for the deities and the nature of the offerings also differ. As an example, the table was only for bloodless libations, for incense, and for gifts of fruit and flowers, or for slaughter of victims of which portions were burnt on it[27]. The temple in Greece was not usually intended for the performance of services or ritual acts. It served chiefly to house the image of the gods and the most precious offerings. Assemblies and services, including sacrifices of all kinds, took place for the most part outside, around the Altar which was their real centre. Therefore, altars were not always associated with temples. There are also traces of altars which are found in the ancient houses[28].

Greeks and Romans made careful distinctions between different Altar forms. There was the raised Altar site where sacrifices to the heavenly gods were performed, the pit that was dug to receive the offerings to the deities of the underworld, and the level ground where gifts to the earth gods were deposited[29]. Egyptian ritual worship included both portable and stationary altars. The former has no sacred function but were simply cult accessories. The later were used in the sun temples. These altars were surrounded by a low wall indicating the special sacred nature of their place during sun rites[30].

The Hebrew term for the Altar is מִזְבֵּחַ (*Mizbeah*), meaning 'a place of sacrificial slaughter', which derived from the word *zabah,* which means 'to slaughter as a sacrifice'. In time, the animal slaughter came to be performed beside, not on, the Altar. Other kinds of oblations offered on the Altar were grain, wine, and incense. The Altar sometimes served as a non-sacrificial function as witness to (Jos 22, 26ff) or denial (I Kgs 1, 50ff) for most crimes except murder. The altars were constructed from unhewn (unpolished) stone, earth, or metal. The tabernacle or the Ark of the Covenant had a bronze-plated Altar for burnt offerings in the court and a gold-plated incense Altar used within the text. Both of these altars were constructed of wood and each was fitted with four rings and two poles for carrying. The Altar for burnt offerings was hollow to make it lighter. Both

---

[27] E. A. GARDNER, «Altar», in *Encyclopedia of Religion and Ethics Vol I*, ed. J. Hastings, T & T Clark, New York 1967, 342-345.
[28] E. A. GARDNER, «Altar», 343.
[29] C. EDSMAN, «Altar», 222.
[30] C. EDSMAN, «Altar», 223.

altars had horns on all the four corners. The Israelite Altar was not of the notion of feeding Yahweh, like pagan religions. The Altars of Yahweh could be erected only in the Promised Land. The Altar represented the place where heaven and earth met, the place from which prayers ascended to God[31].

In Celtic regions, there were many types of Altar. One among them is the Druid Temple Altar, which was destroyed by Ceasar. It seems to be consisted of gloomy wood, written '*structae sacris feralibus arae*' which means 'altars built with offerings to the dead', and artless images of the gods, roughly hewn from logs. The Druidical altars are portable but not indispensable for sacrifice, since the wooden cages filled with men and other victims which are burnt as a holocaust can be offered at any place[32].

There are two types of Altar present in Chinese religions, the Altar of heaven which is very large and the Altar of Earth which is described in the Law of Sacrifices. The Altar of heaven is for the supreme ruler, *Shang-ti*, and the sacrifice is burnt and kept like 'round sacrifice'. The Altar of earth is for the subordinate deities or spirits and the victims were buried and kept like 'spread-out sacrifice'[33]. In the above religions, they use the Altar in their worship with some special intention and specific connotation. However, the Catholic Altar is unique and special. Kelmens Richter affirms that the Christian Altar has nothing to do with the sacrificial altars of other cults[34].

### 1.2.2. HISTORY OF THE CHRISTIAN ALTAR

Jungmann says that in the Church of Christian antiquity, the table on which the material gifts lie is looked upon merely as a technical aid. It is not an Altar at all, in the sense of pre-Christian religions where the gift is hallowed and dedicated to God only when it touches the Altar. Our Gift is intrinsically holy, dedicated to God by its very nature and in the last analysis does not really require an Altar. All the references we possess from third and fourth centuries agree in their account of the Altar. They regard

---

[31] C. EDSMAN, «Altar», 224-225.
[32] L. H. GRAY, «Altar», in *Encyclopedia of Religion and Ethics Vol I*, ed. J. Hastings, T & T Clark, New York 1967, 337.
[33] W. G. WALSHE, «Altar», in *Encyclopedia of Religion and Ethics Vol I*, ed. J. Hastings, T & T Clark, New York 1967, 337.
[34] R. KELMENS, *The Meaning of the Sacramental Symbols: Answers to Today's Questions*, The Liturgical Press, Minnesota 1990, 145.

the Altar not as a part of the permanent structure of the church but only as a simple wooden table which is carried into position by the deacons as occasion dictates[35].

Our knowledge of the history of the Altar and of its exact furnishings reaches back into the 4$^{th}$ century, i.e., into the period when there were stationary Altars which could leave traces. For the preceding period, it is quite obvious that a table must have been present, as at the Last Supper. Facing toward the people or facing with the people toward the East, both arrangements are already found in the 4$^{th}$ century. Then, towards the end of Christian antiquity, the solemnity of divine worship increased. In the East, they strove to shape the earthly liturgy to an image of the heavenly. This goal could be achieved only by increasing its distance from the people. However, with regard to the direction in which the priest and the people faced emphasize on the confrontation of the Altar and the people might have been expected, considering that the Altar had become a stage. However, in fact, the opposite took place[36].

J. B. O'Connell tries to divide the history of the Christian Altar into five periods:

(1) the period up to the 9$^{th}$ century;
(2) from the 9$^{th}$ to the 14$^{th}$ century (the Relic Age);
(3) from the 14$^{th}$ to the beginning of the 19$^{th}$ century (the great reredos period);
(4) the 19$^{th}$ century (the Exposition age);
(5) the 20$^{th}$ century (the reformation period)[37].

At first the Altar used for the celebration of Mass was a very simple one—a small table. It was unconsecrated, unadorned, covered usually with a linen cloth, and with nothing on it, except the bread and wine. It sometimes was made like a tomb, because of the influence from the celebration of the Mass over the tombs of the martyrs in the catacombs or cemeteries[38].

After the Constantinian Peace (4$^{th}$ century) great Altars were erected in the chief churches of Rome and elsewhere. While these were often made of precious

---

[35] J. JUNGMANN, *The Early Liturgy: To the Time of Gregory the Great*, tr. Brunner Francis, University of Notre Dame Press, Indiana 1959, 254.
[36] J. JUNGMANN, «The New Altar», in *Liturgical Arts 37* (1969/2) 36-39, 37.
[37] J. B. O'CONNELL, *Church Building and Furnishing*, 127-132.
[38] J. B. O'CONNELL, *Church Building and Furnishing*, 127.

materials and surmounted by elaborate civories[39], the essential character of the Altar, the simple, unencumbered stone of sacrifice was kept. Until the 9th century only things that were absolutely essential for the celebration of Mass could be placed on the Altar[40].

The 9th century was most importantly the century of widespread popular devotion to relics of the saints. The Altar began to be invaded by reliquaries[41]. This relic invasion was destined to change, little by little, the character, disposition and even the situation of the high Altar. It became necessary to combine the Altar with the relic shrine, and so the table, from being square and small, became oblong and larger. The ever-growing relic shrine led to the abandonment of the *confessio* and to the gradual disappearance of the civory[42]. In the period from the time of St. Benedict in the 6th century until the 11th century, Romanesque architecture emerged. This is also called as the monastic period and because of private Masses, many private Altars were built inside chapels. People's participation was not considered and they were excluded[43].

In the 11th and 12th centuries an elementary type of a fixed frame or shelf (retable) made its appearance. This grew ever bigger and more ornate until it grew into something quite large. The position of the Altar, too, was changed. Instead of being fully detached and standing out clearly in the middle of the sanctuary, it was moved back against the east wall and became more and more merged into its background[44].

The dominant features of the high Altars of the next period (14th to 18th C) were size and over ornamentation. Not only was the permanent adornment of the Altar overdone, but on great feasts temporary adornment (extra candlesticks, reliquaries, church plate, etc.) was piled over the table of the Altar. To add to the complications gradines[45] made their appearance at the end of the 15th century. In this century also the tabernacle became an ordinary feature of the high Altar. The Altar itself, which is the

---

[39] A columned structure above the main altar in the form of canopy made in stone, wood, or metal.
[40] J. B. O'CONNELL, *Church Building and Furnishing*, 128.
[41] Special places where the relics are stored.
[42] J. B. O'CONNELL, *Church Building and Furnishing*, 128.
[43] J. P. BRADLEY, *The Catholic Layman's Library Vol 3*, Goodwill Publishers Inc., North Carolina 1970, 373-374.
[44] J. B. O'CONNELL, *Church Building and Furnishing*, 129.
[45] Shelves at the back of the altar on which candles and flowers are placed.

table of sacrifice, lost all its significance, was dwarfed out of all recognition and ceased to be the focal point of the church[46].

From the 14th and 15th centuries arose the external worship of the reserved Sacrament by expositions and processions, and from the 16th century Benediction was added with the Sacred Host. All through the 17th, 18th and 19th centuries expositions and Benedictions grew ever more frequent. The true character of the high Altar as the place of sacrifice became obscured, the medieval devotion to the Altar disappeared, and the Altar came to be regarded as the 'home of the Blessed Sacrament'[47].

At different periods in the Church's history, since the 8th century, various usages, largely the result of the impact of popular piety, arose that tended to obscure the real nature of an Altar and to diminish the respect it should receive as the consecrated stone of sacrifice. The focal point of the entire edifice became:

(1) relic shrines on and above the Altar (from the 9th C)
(2) retables (from the 11th C)
(3) immense tabernacles (from the 16th C)
(4) exposition thrones (especially in the 18th and 19th C)
(5) gradines (from the 16th C) piled with candlesticks, flower-vases, reliquaries, etc.[48].

The 20th century has seen the development of a movement to restore the real character of the high Altar. First, by having, when possible, a real high Altar, that is, a 'fixed', consecrated Altar. Second, by treating that Altar as the Church desires that it should be treated with Altar cloths and frontal. The Church wanted to restore the dignity of the Altar and the realization of its sacred character by due attention to the essential elements of an Altar[49]. In the same period, sanctuaries were opened up so that the majority of the congregation could see the Altar, though churches were still influenced by both Gothic and classical styles, the Gothic screen was moved back to surround the Altar with a reredos (ornamental screen or wall behind the Altar)[50].

---

[46] J. B. O'CONNELL, *Church Building and Furnishing*, 130.
[47] J. B. O'CONNELL, *Church Building and Furnishing*, 130.
[48] J. B. O'CONNELL, *Church Building and Furnishing*, 127-131
[49] J. B. O'CONNELL, *Church Building and Furnishing*, 132.
[50] J. P. BRADLEY, *The Catholic Layman's Library Vol 3*, 376-377.

## 1.2.3. THE ALTAR IN THE PATRISTIC WRITINGS

In the writings of the Fathers, one can see many theological understanding of the Altar in various aspects. In the beginning, there was an understanding that Christians didn't need an Altar as worship is spiritual and different from the other pagan religions. Minucius Felix says *"Cur nullas aras habent, templa nulla, nulla nota simulacra?"*[51]. That is, there is no material Altar needed for Christians and they tried to see the Altar as something spiritual and identified with the persons living in the community.

*Constitutiones Apostolorum* Chapter II, xxvi, 7-8 say, "αἴ τε χῆραι καὶ οἱ ὀρφανοί εἰς τύπον τοῦ θυσίατήριον λελογίσθωσαν ὑμίν αἴ τε παρθένοι εἰς τύπον τοῦ θυμιατήρου τετιμήσθωσαν καὶ τοῦ θυσιάματος"[52]. The same document encourages the idea that the widow is also a living Altar of God, in Chapter III, vi, 3,

> Γνωριζέτω οὖν ἡ χήρα ὅτι θυσίατήριον ἐστι θεοῦ, καὶ καθήσθω ἐν τῇ οἰκία αὐτῆς, μή μετά τινς προφάσεως ἐν ταῖς τῶν κιστῶν οἰκίαις ἐπί τῷ λαμβάνειν εἰσπορευομένη· οὐδέ γάρ ποτε τό θυσίατήριον τοῦ θεοῦ περιττέχει, ἀλλ' ἐν τόπῳ ἴδρυαι[53].

*De Septem Ordinibus Ecclesiae*, an anonymous treatise on the Church's Seven Offices, is an early 5th century work from Southern Gaul. It says that deacons are Altars. "The deacons are the Altar of Christ, the Altar on which the sacraments are made ready and on which the sacrifice is offered. As you know, what in God's Church can be more venerable than the Altar?"[54].

There was also a development of understanding of the Altar. Origen says in his work 'Homily on the book of Joshua', *"Si Videris neminum ter in anno venire ad*

---

[51] Minucii Felicis, «Octavius», in *Bibliotheca Sanctorum Patrum. Theologiae tironibus et universo clero accommadata* (Scriptores Latini, Series Tertia), ed. I. Vizzini, Ex Officina Typographica Forzani et Socii, Rome 1910, 42.

[52] *Didascalia et Constitutiones Apostolorum* II, xxvi, 7-8, ed. F. X. Funk, Schoeningh, Paderbonae, 1905, 105. tr. "Let the Elders be to you in the likeness of the Apostles, but Orphans and Widows be considered by you in the likeness of an Altar". Quoted from *The Didascalia Apostolorum in English (translated from the Syriac)*, tr. M. D. Gibson, Cambridge University press, London 1903, 48.

[53] *Didascalia et Constitutiones Apostolorum* III, vi, 3, 191. tr. "Let the widow know that she is the Altar of God, and let her constantly sit in her house ; let her not wander and gad about among the houses of believers in order to receive; for the Altar of God does not wander and gad about anywhere, but remains in one place". Quoted from *The Didascalia Apostolorum in English (translated from the Syriac)*, 72.

[54] *De Septem Ordinibus Ecclesiae*, in *Worship in the Early Church: An Anthology of Historical Sources Vol 3*, ed. & tr. L. J. Johnson, Liturgical Press, Minnesota 2009, 175-178, 176.

*conspectum Domini, nec offerre munera in templo, .....sed pretioso Christi sanguine consecrari*"[55]. Origen speaks about the Altar in relation to the blood of Christ.

Optatus of Milevis (ca. 320-385), as a bishop of Milevis in Numedian Africa wrote against the heresies of Donastists, a work called 'Against the Church of Apostates'. "*Quando obtulistis frangere, radere, removere? In quibus et vola popoli et membra Christi portata sunt; quo Deus omnipotens ninvocatus sit...*"[56].

Optatus connects the Altar with the life and being of the Christian. At the same time, there was also simular thinking that the Altar is holy and venerable because it is important in the Liturgy. Ambrose of Milan, in his work, 'Commentary on the Gospel of St. Luke', writes, "It pleased God that we also, when we incense the Altars, when we present the sacrifice, be assisted by the angel, or rather that the angel make himself visible. For you cannot doubt that the angel is there when Christ is there"[57]. By this Ambrose affirms that Christ is present in the Altar.

The Canons of Father Athanasius, Canon No. 7 says, "...Because the Lord stands over the Altar, so the Altar's vessels are spiritual, being neither silver nor gold, neither stone nor wood, just as the bread and wine, before being raised over the Altar, are bread and wine. Yet after they are raised over the Altar, they are no longer bread and wine but are the life-giving and divine Body and Blood so that those receiving them do not die but live forever. The same is no less true of the Altar, whether it be of wood, stone, gold, or silver. It is not mortal as its former substance, but being spiritual it lives

---

[55] ORIGÈNE, «Homilia II», in *Homélies sur Josué*, ed. A. Jaubert, (Sources Chrétiennes 71) Paris 1960, 116-123, 116. tr. "You see the pagans come to faith, Churches being built up, Altars sprinkled no longer with the blood of oxen but consecrated by the precious blood of Christ". Quoted from ORIGEN, «Homily on Joshua», in *Worship in the Early Church: An Anthology of Historical Sources Vol 1*, ed. & tr. L. J. Johnson, Liturgical Press, Minnesota 2009, 246-257, 251.

[56] OPTAT DE MILÈVE, «Liber Sextus», in *Traité Contre Les Donatistes*, ed. M. Labrousse, (Sources Chrétiennes 413) Paris 1996, 160-191, 160. tr. "What is so sacrilegious as to break, scrape, remove God's Altar on which you yourselves had once offered, on which both the prayers of the people and the members of Christ had been held, where God Almighty has been invoked, where God Almighty has been invoked, where the Holy Spirit has been requested and has descended, from which many have received the pledge of eternal salvation, the safeguard of the faith, and hope of resurrection?". Quoted from OPTATUS, *The Work of St. Optatus: Against Donatists*, tr. O. R. V. Phillips, Longmans, Green & Co., London 1917, 246.

[57] AMBROSE, «Commentary on the Gospel of St. Luke», in *Worship in the Early Church: An Anthology of Historical Sources Vol 2*, ed. & tr. L. J. Johnson, Liturgical Press, Minnesota 2009, 12-80, 19.

forever"[58]. The presence of Christ and the holiness of the Altar were the ideas we can see in these Fathers.

At the same time, the Eastern Church Fathers also contributed for the understanding of Altar. John Chrysostom of Syria (ca. 347-407),in his 'Homilies on Second Letter to the Corinthians' in 'Homily 18' writes, "the Church is to dwell as one household; it is to come together as one body just as there is but one baptism, one table, one font, one creation, and one Father. Why, then, are we divided when such great things unite us?"[59]. According to him, the Altar is a uniting element. Balai, a 5th century Syrian poet (+ 460) in his 'Hymn for the Dedication of a New Church' writes:

> His Altar is ready and he takes his meal with us;
> His glory is offered to men, and they take their place at table;
> We eat with him at our table
> One day he will eat with us at his[60].

From the theological poem of Balai, we can come to know the meal aspect and the communion aspect of the Altar and there was also the idea of veneration of the Altar. Gregory of Nazianus (ca. 329-390), in his 'Sermon on the day of Lights on which our Lord was baptized', writes about the Altar:

> The Altar, at which we are standing, is holy. Yet by nature, it is ordinary, in no way differing from other stone slabs that built up our walls and adorn our pavements. But because the holy table is consecrated and dedicated to the worship of God and has been blessed, it is a spotless Altar which no longer is touched by all but only by the priests as they venerate it[61].

He brings out the holiness of the Altar and the veneration to it. Narsai of Nisibus(ca. 399-503), write in his 'Homilies' when he explains the Eucharistic sacrifice, "the Altar stands crowned with beauty and splendor, and upon it are the Gospel of Life and the adorable wood, that is, the Cross"[62]. He brings out the splendour of the Altar

---

[58] CANONS OF FATHER ATHANASIUS, in *Worship in the Early Church: An Anthology of Historical Sources Vol 2*, ed. & tr. L. J. Johnson, Liturgical Press, Minnesota 2009, 415-422, 416.

[59] JOHN CHRYSOSTOM, «Homilies on Second Letter to Corinthians», in *Worship in the Early Church: An Anthology of Historical Sources Vol 2*, ed. & tr. L. J. Johnson, Liturgical Press, Minnesota 2009, 171-211, 185.

[60] BALAI, «Hymn for the Dedication of a New Church», in *Worship in the Early Church: An Anthology of Historical Sources Vol 3*, ed. & tr. L. J. Johnson, Liturgical Press, Minnesota 2009, 287-288, 288.

[61] GREGORY OF NAZIANUS, «Sermon on the day of Lights on which our Lord was baptized», in *Worship in the Early Church: An Anthology of Historical Sources Vol 2*, ed. & tr. L. J. Johnson, Liturgical Press, Minnesota 2009, 151-159, 155.

[62] NARSAI OF NISIBUS, «Homilies», in *Worship in the Early Church: An Anthology of Historical Sources Vol 3*, ed. & tr. L. J. Johnson, Liturgical Press, Minnesota 2009, 288-305, 292-293.

and he adds, "... the venerable Altar is a symbol of the throne of the Great and Glorious one..."[63]. Both his texts talk about the beauty of Altar and the symbolism as a throne of God. Theodore of Mopuestia (Ca. 350-428) in his 'Homily on Eucharist' writes, "When they bring out the bread, they place it on the holy Altar for the perfect representation of the passion. In this regard we believe that the Altar upon which Christ, having suffered, is placed resembles a type of a tomb"[64]. According to him, the Altar represents the tomb of Christ where he was buried and from where he resurrected.

### 1.2.4. THE ALTAR IN CONCILIAR AND OTHER CHURCH DOCUMENTS

Since the proclamation of *Sacrosanctum Concilium*, there has been a more radical change in the arrangement of our churches than we have seen for centuries. Yet the Constitution itself says very little about such changes, and in chapter 7, on Sacred Art and Furnishings, the Fathers of the Council contented themselves with affirming their recognition of the ministry of the artist and with a reminder of the need to make the place of worship really suitable for its purpose[65].

*Sacrosanctum Concilium* 124 says, "*In aedificandis vero sacris aedibus, diligenter curetur ut ad liturgicas actiones exsequendas et ad fidelium actuosam participationem obtinendam idoneae sint*"[66]. This article brings out the importance of active participation in the Liturgy and the building of the sanctuary should be helpful for the faithful to celebrate the liturgy. In *Sacrosanctum Concilium* 128 we see the following instruction regarding Altar,

> Canones et statuta ecclesiastica, quae rerum externarum ad sacrum cultum pertinentium apparatum spectant, praesertim quoad aedium sacrarum dignam et aptam constructionem, Altarium formam et aedificationem, tabernaculi eucharistici nobilitatem, dispositionem et securitatem, baptisterii convenientiam et honorem, necnon congruentem sacrarum imaginum, decorationis et ornatus rationem, una cum libris liturgicis ad normam art. 25 quam primum recognoscantur: quae liturgiae instauratae minus congruere

---

[63] NARSAI OF NISIBUS, «Homilies», 290.
[64] THEODORE OF MOPUSUETIA, «Homily on Eucharist», in *Worship in the Early Church: An Anthology of Historical Sources Vol 3*, ed. & tr. L. J. Johnson, Liturgical Press, Minnesota 2009, 246-275, 262.
[65] BRADLEY J. P., *The Catholic Layman's Library Vol 3*, 369.
[66] CONCILIUM OECUMENICUM VATICANUM II, Constitutio de Sacra Liturgia *Sacrosanctum Concilium 124*, AAS 56 (1964) 131.

videntur, emendentur aut aboleantur; quae vero ipsi favent, retineantur vel introducantur[67].

The above article quoted, asks for a well-planned and worthy construction of Altar. Cardinal G. Lercaro, in his letter to presidents of the conference of bishops 'On Furthering Liturgical Reform', writes about the Altar facing people and the pastoral advantages of this practice. He also added that the construction of Altars facing the people is therefore desirable in new churches; elsewhere it will be achieved gradually through seriously studied adaptations that take all values into account[68].

*Intructio*[69], on the orderly carrying out of the Constitution on the Liturgy, 26 September 1964, encourages the designing of churches and Altars to facilitate active participation. Number 90 says, "*In ecclesiis noviter erigendis, reficiendis aut aptandis sedulo curetur ut idoneae evadant ad actiones sacras celebrandas iuxta veram ipsarum naturam, et ad fidelium actuosam participationem obtinendam*"[70].

This is the first explicit instruction which makes an appeal about the free standing Altar and *Altar versus populum*[71]. Number 91 of *Intructio* says, "*Praestat ut Altare maius exstruatur a pariete seiunctum, ut facile circumiri et in eo celebratio*

---

[67] CONCILIUM OECUMENICUM VATICANUM II, Constitutio de Sacra Liturgia *Sacrosanctum Concilium 128*, 132. tr. "Along with the revision of the liturgical books, as laid down in Art. 25, there is to be an early revision of the canons and ecclesiastical statutes which govern the provision of material things involved in sacred worship. These laws refer especially to the worthy and well planned construction of sacred buildings, the shape and construction of Altars, the nobility, placing, and safety of the Eucharistic tabernacle, the dignity and suitability of the baptistery, the proper ordering of sacred images, embellishments, and vestments. Laws which seem less suited to the reformed liturgy are to be brought into harmony with it, or else abolished; and any which are helpful are to be retained if already in use, or introduced where they are lacking". Quoted from VATICAN COUNCIL II, The Constitution on the Sacred Liturgy, *Sacrosanctum Concilium*: in *The Conciliar and Post Conciliar Documents* 1, ed. A. Flannery, St. Paul Publications, Bombay 1988, 36.

[68] CONSILIUM, «Letter *Le renouveau liturgique* of Cardinal G. Lercaro to presidents of the conference of bishops, on furthering liturgical reform (30 June 1965)», in *Documents on the Liturgy 1963 – 1979, Conciliar, Papal, and Curial Texts*, The Liturgical Press, Minnesota 1982, 117-122.

[69] SACRA CONGREGATIO RITUUM, *Instructio, ad exsecutionem constitutionis de sacra liturgia recte ordinandam, AAS 56* (1964) 877-900.

[70] SACRA CONGREGATIO RITUUM, *Instructio 90, ad exsecutionem constitutionis de sacra liturgia recte ordinandam*, 897. tr. "In building new Churches or restoring and adapting old ones every care is to be taken that they are suited to celebrating liturgical services authentically and that they ensure active participation by the faithful". Quoted from SC RITES (Consilium), «Instruction (first) *Inter Oecumenici*, on the orderly carrying out of the Constitution on the Liturgy, 26 September 1964», in *Documents on the Liturgy 1963 – 1979, Conciliar, Papal, and Curial Texts*, The Liturgical Press, Minnesota 1982, 88-110, 108.

[71] J. JUNGMANN, «The New Altar», 36.

*versus populum peragi possit; in sacra autem aede eum occupet locum, ut revera centrum sit quo totius congregationis fidelium attentio sponte convertatur"*[72].

In the *Decretum*[73] from the Congregation for Sacraments and Divine Worship for *Ordo Dedicationis Ecclesiae et Altaris* 1977, says, "*...Altare vero, quod plebs sancta circumdat ut sacrificium dominicum participet et caelesti reficiatus convivio, signum exsistit Christi, qui sacerdos, hostia, Altare est sui ipsius sacrificii*"[74]. In the instructions given in *Ordo Dedicationis Ecclesiae et Altaris* 1977, we get a high theology and the understanding of the Altar in the church, especially the fourth chapter on Rite of Dedication of an Altar[75]. This chapter brings out the dignity of the Altar and exhorts that all the Christians are spiritual Altars of God. The Altar is a sign of Christ and it also honors Martyrs. It will be dealt elaborately in the second chapter where the gestures, veneration and symbolism with regard to the Altar are dealt with.

In the General Instruction of the Roman Missal[76], numbers 296-308 clearly speaks about the nature, function and arrangement of the Altar. In the Ceremonial of Bishops[77], No. 48 insists that the consecration of the Altar according to the norms and No. 72-73 exhort the reverence toward the Altar. The United States Bishops' Conference issued a document called '*Environment and Art in Catholic Worship*' in

---

[72] SACRA CONGREGATIO RITUUM, *Instructio 91, ad exsecutionem constitutionis de sacra liturgia recte ordinandam*, 898. tr. "The main Altar should preferably be freestanding, to permit walking around it celebration facing the people. Its location in the place of worship should be truly central so that the attention of the whole congregation naturally focuses there. Choice of materials for the construction and adornment of the Altar is to respect the prescriptions of law. The sanctuary area is to be spacious enough to accommodate the sacred rites". Quoted from SC RITES (Consilium), «Instruction (first) *Inter Oecumenici,* on the orderly carrying out of the Constitution on the Liturgy, 26 September 1964», 108.
[73] DECRETUM (Prot. No. CD 300/77), in *Ordo Dedicationis Ecclesiae et Altaris, Pontificale Romanum, Ex Decreto Sacrosancti Ecumenici Concili Vaticani II Instauratum Auctoritate Pauli PP. VI Promulgatum*, Typis Polyglottis Vaticanis, Romae 1977, 5-6.
[74] DECRETUM (Prot. No. CD 300/77), 5. tr. "And the Altar of a Church, where the holy people of God gathers to take part in the Lord's sacrifice and to be refreshed by the heavenly meal, stands as a sign of Christ himself, who is the priest, the victim, and the Altar of his own sacrifice". Quoted from G. S. DUNCAN, *The Church Building as a Sacred Place: Beauty, Transcendence, and the Eternal*, Liturgy Training Publications, Illinois 2012, 20.
[75] *Ordo Dedicationis Ecclesiae et Altaris, Pontificale Romanum, Ex Decreto Sacrosancti Ecumenici Concili Vaticani II Instauratum Auctoritate Pauli PP. VI Promulgatum*, 82-111.
[76] *Institutio Generalis Missalis Romani No. 296-308*, in *Missale Romanum Ex Decreto Sacrosancti Oecumenici Concilii Vaticani II, Instauratum auctoritate Pauli PP.VI promulgatum Ioannis Pauli PP. II cura recognitum*, Typis Vaticanis, Citta del Vaticano ³2008, 17- 86.
[77] INTERNATIONAL COMMISSION ON ENGLISH IN THE LITURGY, *Ceremonial of Bishops: Revised by Decree of the Second Vatican Ecumenical Council and Published by Authority of Pope John Paul II*, The Liturgical Press, Minnesota 1989, 30 & 37.

1978. This had a profound impact on the building and renovation of parish churches in the United States. Twenty-two years after the publication of *'Environment and Art'*, the bishops of the United States presented a new document on church art and architecture that builds on and replaces 'Environment and Art' and addresses the needs of the next generation of parishes engaged in building or renovating churches. 'Built of Living Stones' reflects our understanding of the liturgy, of the role and importance of the church art and architecture, and of the integral roles of the local parish and the diocese that enter into a building project. In this document, we see good understanding of the Altar and its settings. Especially, No. 56-60 and No. 245-246 deal with the understanding and building of the Altar[78].

## 1.3. CENTRALITY OF THE ALTAR IN THE LITURGY

The Altar is the primary symbol of a Church and is, accordingly, the central feature. Although not necessarily the geometric centre of the sanctuary, it is both a major point of activity and commands the building, because of its threefold symbol: Christ's body, the Altar of sacrifice, and the table of the Last Supper[79]. The Altar occupies the most important place in the Church, since upon it the Holy Sacrifice of the Mass, about which Catholic faith centres, is celebrated[80]. There is no place set apart for celebrating the liturgy unless it has an Altar. From earliest times the Altar has been the hierarchical centre and the focus of the liturgy and a representation of Christ[81]. The lights directed on the Altar gives the proper emphasis on the liturgical dignity and centrality of the place of Eucharistic worship[82].

### 1.3.1. TABERNACLE AND THE ALTAR

The ancient Fathers of the Church assert more than once: "This Altar is an object of wonder: by nature it is stone, but it is made holy when it receives the body of

---

[78] UNITED STATES CONFERENCE OF CATHOLIC BISHOPS, *Built of Living Stones (2000)*, in The Liturgy Documents Vol I, ed., David Lysik, Liturgy Training Publications, Chicago 2004, 417-498.
[79] J. P. BRADLEY, *The Catholic Layman's Library Vol 3*, 392.
[80] M. NICHOLAS, *Altars according to the Code of Canon Law*, vii.
[81] G. S. DUNCAN, *The Church Building as a Sacred Place: Beauty, Transcendence, and the Eternal*, 20.
[82] D. GODFREY, «The Place of Liturgical Worship», in *The Church and the Liturgy Vol 2*, ed., J. Wagner, Paulist Press, New Jersey 1964, 93.

Christ"[83]. The tabernacle is rightly seen as an extension of the sacrifice of the Mass, a house for the reservation of Christ's Body offered on the Altar. The conciliar documents see the tabernacle as an important element to the definition of the Church. *Presbyterorum Ordinis* 5 says, "*Domus orationis in qua Sanctissima Eucharistia celebratur et servatur, fidelesque congregantur, et in qua praesentia Filii Dei Salvatoris nostri in ara sacrificali pro nobis oblati, in auxilium atque solatium fidelium colitur, nitida, orationi et sacris sollemnibus apta esse debet*"[84].

As symbol and presence of the Lord, it seems natural that the Altar and the tabernacle should be readily identifiable upon entering the church building. Duncan writes that the tabernacle should be designed and constructed in a manner commensurate with its high status and inherent dignity, and located in a position that engenders the respect of the faithful. The Altar, which represents Christ who is the perfect Altar of sacrifice, and the tabernacle, which houses Christ's Real Presence, are rightly placed in the sanctuary and seen as interrelated. Spiritually, the design of the church building begins with the Altar, then moves to the tabernacle, and then flows from them. This can be thought of as analogous to the Holy Spirit, who proceeds from the Father and the Son. The tabernacle and the Altar are both appropriate foci of the church building, and thus their location is most appropriately on the central axis of the church, allowing their interdependence to be made evident[85].

According to canon law, Can. 938 § 2, "*Tabernaculum, in quo sanctissima Eucharistia asservatur, situm sit in aliqua ecclesiae vel oratorii parte insigni, conspicua, decore ornata, ad orationem apta*"[86]. The tabernacle will be given similar

---

[83] M. C. IGNAZIO, *The Dedication of a Church and an Altar: A Theological Commentary*, United States Catholic Conference, Washington 1980, 32.
[84] CONCILIUM OECUMENICUM VATICANUM II, Decretum de Presbyterorum Ministerio et Vita *Presbyterorum Ordinis 5*, *AAS* 58 (1966) 997. tr. "The house of prayer in which the Most Holy Eucharist is celebrated and reserved, where the faithful gather and where the presence of the Son of God, our Savior, offered for us on the Altar of sacrifice bestows strength and blessings on the faithful, must be spotless and suitable for prayer and sacred functions". Quoted from VATICAN COUNCIL II, *Presbyterorum Ordinis*: in *The Conciliar and Post Conciliar Documents* 1, 872.
[85] G. S. Duncan, *The Church Building as a Sacred Place: Beauty, Transcendence, and the Eternal*, 26.
[86] *Code of Canon Law Annotated*, ed. E. Caparros, Wilson & Lafleus Limitee, Montreal 1993, 599.

prominence as the Altar, because it is the location of the abiding presence of Christ, who said, "I am with you always, until the end of the age" (Mt 28, 20)[87].

In the 16th Century, the tabernacle was generally placed on the main Altar as a reaction to the denial of the real presence by the Reformers. The Altar served as a highly ornamented throne for the tabernacle and even on the side Altars, non-functional decorative tabernacles were placed[88]. Then in the following centuries it has become mandatory that the tabernacle is placed on the Altar. It took few centuries to restore the real dignity and nature of Altar. In 1956 Pope Pius XII, when he spoke to the participants of the International Pastoral-Liturgical Congress of Assisi, said, "The Altar surpasses the Tabernacle, because on it is offered the sacrifice of the Lord. The tabernacle doubtless possesses the *Sacramentum permanens*; but it is not an *Altare permanens*, because it is only during the celebration of the holy mass that Christ offers himself, on the Altar- not after, not outside of mass. In the tabernacle, on the other hand, he is present as long as the consecrated species remain, without however offering himself perpetually"[89].

*Sacrosanctum Concilium* in article No. 128, calls for the revision of canons and ecclesiastical statutes which govern the provision of material things involved in sacred worship[90]. There were many discussions in transferring the tabernacle from the Altar to a suitable place. At last, we see in GIRM, No. 315:

> Ratione signi magis congruit ut in Altari in quo Missa celebratur non sit tabernaculum in quo Sanctissima Eucharistia asservatur. Praestat proinde tabernaculum collocari, de iudicio Episcopi dioecesani: (a). aut in presbyterio, extra Altare celebrationis, forma et loco magis convenientibus, non excluso vetere Altari quod ad celebrationem amplius non adhibetur. (b). aut etiam in aliquo sacello ad privatam fidelium adorationem et precationem idoneo, quod sit cum ecclesia organice coniunctum et christifidelibus conspicuum[91].

---

[87] G. S. Duncan, *The Church Building as a Sacred Place: Beauty, Transcendence, and the Eternal*, 26.
[88] D. GODFREY, «Altar and Tabernacle», in *Worship 40* (1966/8) 490-509, 492.
[89] D. GODFREY, «Altar and Tabernacle», 494.
[90] CONCILIUM OECUMENICUM VATICANUM II, Constitutio de Sacra Liturgia *Sacrosanctum Concilium 128*, 131.
[91] *Institutio Generalis Missalis Romani No. 315*, in *Missale Romanum Ex Decreto Sacrosancti Oecumenici Concilii Vaticani II, Instauratum auctoritate Pauli PP.VI promulgatum Ioannis Pauli PP. II cura recognitum*, 72. tr. "It is more appropriate as a sign that on an Altar on which Mass is celebrated there not be a tabernacle in which the Most Holy Eucharist is reserved.128 Consequently, it is preferable that the tabernacle be located, according to the judgement of the Diocesan Bishop: a. either in the sanctuary, apart from the Altar of celebration, in a appropriate form and place, not excluding its being

There are proper Guidelines in the document 'Built of Living Stones: Art, Architecture, and Worship' issued by the United States Conference of Catholic Bishops in 2000, for the placement of tabernacle. Especially No. 70-80, speaks about the proper place for the tabernacle[92]. One can see that the Altar and tabernacle are very much connected and yet the Altar is the centre of the liturgical worship.

## 1.3.2. ORIENTATION AND THE ALTAR

In the reform of liturgical worship implemented since *Sacrosanctum Concilium*, nothing is more striking, apart from the universal adoption of the vernacular, than the almost equally universal adoption of a Eucharistic celebration *versus populum*[93]. Jungmann says the "Altar is either facing people or facing away? History indicates that both practices were in use from the very start, at least in the vicinity of Rome. Even today, they are both countenanced in the *Missale Romanum*"[94]. There is also the question of facing east for prayer. The phrase *ad orientem* originally meant that church buildings and those who shared in the Eucharist faced east because that was understood to be the direction from which Christ would return at the second coming. The logic was that, since the sun rises in the east that is where Christ will come from at the end of time as the Light of the world[95]. There are various discussions on this issue.

The Jews in the synagogue, hearing the word of God, looked at the Ark and beyond the Ark at the Jerusalem Holy of Holies, which it evoked. The Christians in their churches, hearing the Word, are led by it from the Ark to the Altar. Beyond the Altar itself, they look toward no other earthly place but only toward the rising sun as toward the symbol of *Sol justitiae* they are expecting[96]. And the *Apostolic Constitution*, also

---

positioned on an old Altar no longer used for celebration (No. 303); b. or even in some chapel suitable for the private adoration and prayer of the faithful129 and organically connected to the Church and readily noticeable by the Christian faithful". Quoted from *General Instruction of the Roman Missal: Liturgy Documentary Series 2*, tr. International Committee on English in the Liturgy, United states Conference of Catholic Bishops Publishing, Washington 2003, 107.

[92] UNITED STATES CONFERENCE OF CATHOLIC BISHOPS, *Built of Living Stones: Art, Architecture, and Worship*, United States Catholic Conference Inc., Washington 2000, 28-30.
[93] C. NAPIER, «The Altar in the Contemporary Church», in in *The Clergy Review 57* (1972/8) 624-632, 624.
[94] J. JUNGMANN, *The Mass of the Roman Rite: Its Origin and Development Vol I*, tr. Francis A. Brunner, Christian Classic Inc., Maryland 1986, 255.
[95] W. I. KEVIN, *Models of the Eucharist*, Paulist Press, New York 2005, 206.
[96] L. BOUYER, *Liturgy and Architecture*, University of Notre Dame Press, Indiana 1967, 31.

from Syria, indicates that the people are to rise and face the east for the prayer of the faithful.

> Let a place be reserved for the Elders in the midst of the eastern part of the House, and let the throne of the Bishop be placed amongst them ; let the Elders sit with him ; but also at the other eastern side of the house let the laymen sit ; for thus it is required that the Elders should sit at the eastern side of the house with the Bishops, and afterwards the laymen, and next the women : that when you stand to pray the rulers may stand first, afterwards the laymen, and then the women also, for towards the East it is required that you should pray[97].

J. H. Miller in his article affirms that the church should be built in the direction of the East and how all should face the East at prayer and several Fathers of the East like Clement of Alexandria and Origen explain this custom[98].

Pope Benedict wrote in favour of *ad orientem*. In his work 'The Spirit of the Liturgy' he affirms that when one turns to the East, both priest and faithful are turning towards the Jesus of the Second Coming. It is not a return to the past but a bold march forward to eternity[99]. J. A. Jungmann also had the idea of the priest and people facing in the same direction would be a good practice showing that they are in procession towards the Lord[100]. However, Kevin questions this view saying,

> When Mass was celebrated *ad orientem* in the patristic era, the posture of the congregation was standing, everyone listened to the words of the priest, especially during the Eucharistic prayer, and there were no elevations at the words of institution. If one determines that the *ad orientem* precedent should be imitated does that mean that these other practices should be revised as well?[101]

This is all the more surprising since in the documents including the Constitution of the Sacred Liturgy, there is strictly not a word about *altar versus populum*[102]. From the history of the church architecture, there can be some clarifications. From the 4th century to the 6th century it was the practice in all greater churches to

---

[97] *The Didascalia Apostolorum in English (translated from the Syriac)*, 65.
[98] J. H. MILLER, «Altar facing the people: fact or fable?», in *Worship* 33 (1959/2) 85.
[99] J. RATZINGER, *The Spirit of the Liturgy*, tr. John Saward, Ignatius Press, San Francisco 2000, 74-80.
[100] J. JUNGMANN, «The New Altar», 36-40.
[101] W. I. KEVIN, *Models of the Eucharist*, 207.
[102] J. JUNGMANN, «The New Altar», 36.

celebrate mass facing the congregation. Even in private houses, or in chapels, or even in the catacombs the celebrant used to face the people[103].

According to J. B. O'Connell, the practice of celebrating with the celebrant's back turned to the congregation gradually arose with the change in the position of the people, desiring to face East at prayer, with the growth of the number of priests for missions and in monasteries and with the multiplication of the Masses 'for a private intention' and private masses for the dead (these masses were said in small chapels, not at the high Altar). The practice of saying Mass back to the people, at side Altars, gradually spread to the high Altar[104]. Meanwhile, in the course of history:

> the disappearance of the *'confessio'*, the change in the position of the throne from apse to the Gospel side of the chancel (in some places as early as the 9th and 10th centuries), the appearance of large reliquaries on or behind the Altar, the advent of retable and gradines (from the 11th century), and the placing of the tabernacle on the Altar (from the end of 13th century), all tended to drive the Altar from its forward position to the back of the apse, and not infrequently it was embedded in the very structure of the apse (especially in 16th and 17th centuries)[105].

The position of the Altar was also affected by the question of orientation and the change in the relative position of the priest and people for celebration of Mass[106]. P. C. Bussard says that having the Mass facing the people was the usual custom for a great many centuries and is quite evident from three things. First, that the bishop had his throne in the apse where the Altar now commonly stands against the wall; second, that the rubrics for incensing the Altar supposed that the priest walked completely around it; and third, that the place where the sub-deacon stood was on the other side of the Altar facing the priest and not behind the deacon[107]. Moreover, when we practically look at the celebration of the Eucharist, to celebrate Mass facing people is more logical especially concerning the parts directly addressed to them. As it makes it easier to see and hear the celebrant, it renders active participation by the people more feasible[108].

---

[103] J. B. O'CONNELL, *Church Building and Furnishing*, 153-154.
[104] J. B. O'CONNELL, *Church Building and Furnishing*, 154.
[105] J. B. O'CONNELL, *Church Building and Furnishing*, 151.
[106] J. B. O'CONNELL, *Church Building and Furnishing*, 151.
[107] P. C. BUSSARD, «Altar Alteration», in *Orate Fratres 13* (1938) 66.
[108] J. B. O'CONNELL, *Church Building and Furnishing*, 154-155.

Cardinal Lercaro in his letter to the *International Bishop's Conference of January 25, 1966*, maintained that prudence must be the guide in the renewal of Altars, and said,

> The turning of the Altar to the people is not indispensable for a living participation in the liturgy. In entire service of the word in the mass is celebrated at the priest's seat or at the pulpit, and therefore facing the congregation. With regard to the participation in the Eucharist, public address systems, which have become common now, allow sufficient participation[109].

The only explicit instruction to which appeal can be made is contained in the *Instructio* issued under date of September 26, 1965, two years after the Constitution on the Sacred Liturgy. Number 91 of this *Instructio* says, "the high Altar is to be separated from the rear wall so that one can (*possit*) walk around it without difficulty and celebrate at it facing the people"[110]. The new GIRM No. 299 says:

> Altare maius exstruatur a pariete seiunctum, ut facile circumiri et in eo celebratio versus populum peragi possit, quod expedit ubicumque possibile sit. Altare eum autem occupet locum, ut revera centrum sit ad quod totius congregationis fidelium attentio sponte convertatur. De more sit fixum et dedicatum[111].

What is underscored when the Eucharist is celebrated facing the people is that aspect of the Eucharistic theology that emphasizes it as a sacred meal[112]. Facing the people would obviously bring the Altar much closer to them[113].

### 1.3.3. RELICS AND THE ALTAR

The cult of the martyrs dates from the 2nd century. At that time, their 'relics' meant the entire body of the saint, and was honoured at the place of its burial by a

---

[109] CONSILIUM, «Letter *Le renouveau liturgique* of Cardinal G. Lercaro to presidents of the conference of bishops, on furthering liturgical reform (30 June 1965)», in *Documents on the Liturgy 1963 – 1979, Conciliar, Papal, and Curial Texts*, The Liturgical Press, Minnesota 1982 117-122, 119.

[110] SC RITES (Consilium), «Instruction (first) *Inter Oecumenici*, on the orderly carrying out of the Constitution on the Liturgy, 26 September 1964», 108.

[111] *Institutio Generalis Missalis Romani No. 299*, in *Missale Romanum Ex Decreto Sacrosancti Oecumenici Concilii Vaticani II, Instauratum auctoritate Pauli PP.VI promulgatum Ioannis Pauli PP. II cura recognitum*, 68-69. tr. "The Altar should be built separate from the wall, in such a way that it is possible to walk around it easily and that Mass can be celebrated at it facing the people, which is desirable wherever possible. Moreover, the Altar should occupy a place where it is truly the centre toward which the attention of the whole congregation of the faithful naturally turns.The Altar should usually be fixed and dedicated". *General Instruction of the Roman Missal: Liturgy Documentary Series 2*, 100-101.

[112] W. I. KEVIN, *Models of the Eucharist*, 207.

[113] D. GODFREY, «The Place of Liturgical Worship», 94.

*tropaeum* or *martyrium* constructed over it[114]. By the 6th or 7th century, these relics were dismembered and enclosed in the Altar itself, just as is prescribed for every Altar today[115]. At first the relics of martyrs were under Altars (in a crypt or *confessio*); then came – in the 6th and 7th centuries – the practice of sometimes putting relics, in a casket, into the Altar, which was taken as a kind of tomb. The 8th and 9th centuries saw the beginning of our modern usage of inserting small relics into the table of the Altar; and at the same period, it was allowed to place reliquaries on the Altar during the celebration of Mass[116]. The high honor paid to the relics led to another step in the 9th century in favor of reliquaries or relic-shrines[117]. Finally came the practice of putting relics for veneration over and behind Altars[118].

Enrico Mazza in his book 'The Celebration of the Eucharist' treats in detail the history of relics with regard to the Altar and Eucharistic celebration[119]. He explains the practice of burial of relics in the Altar along with particles of the Holy Eucharist. According to him, in 12th Century, particles of the Holy Eucharist were also kept with the relics to emphasize the holiness and sacredness of the Altar and in the process of history, it has stopped[120].

The *sepulchre* was generally placed in the middle of the Altar table towards the front edge, but, in a 'fixed' Altar, it could also be placed midway between the table and the floor, either in the front or back of the Altar. Relics were enclosed in the *sepulchre* at the consecration, even though a body of a saint is entombed beneath the Altar. The '*Sepulchre*' must be capable of containing the reliquary, three grains of incense and the attestation of the consecration[121]. In the West, it became the custom to set up the Altar over the tomb of a martyr, which led to the evolution of the *confessio*, i.e., the crypt

---

[114] J. B. O'CONNELL, *Church Building and Furnishing*, 128.
[115] J. JUNGMANN, *The Mass of the Roman Rite: Its Origin and Development Vol I*, 258.
[116] J. B. O'CONNELL, *Church Building and Furnishing*, 128.
[117] J. JUNGMANN, *The Mass of the Roman Rite: Its Origin and Development Vol I*, 258.
[118] J. B. O'CONNELL, *Church Building and Furnishing*, 128.
[119] E. MAZZA, *The Celebration of the Eucharist: Origin of the Rite and Development of its Interpretation*, tr. M. J. O'Connell, The Liturgical Press, Minnesota 1999, 225-236.
[120] E. MAZZA, *The Celebration of the Eucharist: Origin of the Rite and Development of its Interpretation*, 229-230.
[121] J. B. O'CONNELL, *Church Building and Furnishing*, 142-149.

beneath the high Altar where a martyr's relics are enshrined, chiefly in the Roman basilicas[122].

M. Nicholas, the author of '*Altars according to the Code of Canon Law*', says that in early history the faithful were commanded to assemble in the cemeteries for the reading of the Holy Scripture and recitation of psalms in honour of the martyrs and saints, and for the faithful departed; and also to offer the Eucharistic sacrifice in churches and cemeteries[123].

Paulinus of Nola (ca. 355-431) in his 'Letter to Severus' writes a beautiful theological poem about Altar and martyrs:

> The holy Altar conceals a divine union.
> > Martyrs together with the holy cross are placed here.
> The whole martyrdom of Christ the Saviour is gathered here,
> > The cross, the body, the blood, the martyr, Divinity itself.
> God always preserves the divine gifts to you.
> > Where Christ is, there the Spirit and the Father are.
> Thus where the cross is, so too is the martyr because
> > The martyr's cross is the holy reason for the saint's martyrdom.
> When cross has given us the food of life, it has given a crown
> > Whereby his servants share in the Lord.
> The flesh that I eat is nailed to the cross.
> > His blood, by which I drink life and wash my heart flows from the cross[124].

St. Augustine who thus writes of the Altar erected on the site of the martyrdom of St. Cyprian:

> Mensa Deo constructa est; et tamen mensa dicitur Cypriani, non quia ibi est unquam Cyprianus epulatus, sed quia ibi est immolatus, et quia ipsa immolatione sun paravit hanc mensam, non in qua pascat sive pascatur, sed in qua sacrificium Deo, cui et ipse oblatus est, offeratur[125].

St. Ambrose says "*Succedant victimae triumphales in locum ubi Christus hostia est. Sed ille super Altare, quo pro omnibus passus est. Isti sub Altari, qui illius*

---

[122] J. P. BRADLEY, *The Catholic Layman's Library Vol 3*, 373.
[123] M. NICHOLAS, *Altars according to the Code of Canon Law*, 26.
[124] PAULINUS, «Letter to Severus», in *Worship in the Early Church: An Anthology of Historical Sources Vol 3*, ed. & tr. L. J. Johnson, Liturgical Press, Minnesota 2009, 104-109, 105.
[125] AUGUSTINUS, «Sermo CCCX: In Natali Cypriani Martyris II», in *Collectio selecta SS. Ecclesiae Patrum complectens Exquitissima opera tum Dogmatica et Moralia, tum Apologetica et Oratoria: Sancti Aurelii Augustini Hipponensis Episcopi Operum Pars IV. Opera Oratoria*, ed. D. A. Caillau, Parent-Desbarres, Paris 1838, 101-103, 102.

*redempti sunt passione*"[126]. The same is quoted in the 'Rite of Dedication of a Church and an Altar' No. 5[127], "Let the triumphant victims take their place where Christ is the victim. He who suffered for all is above the Altar; those redeemed by his sufferings are beneath the Altar"[128].

St. Augustine erected an Altar over the relics of St. Stephen, which indicates the practice in Northern Africa. "*Nos enim in isto loco non aram fecimus Stephano, sed de reliquiis Stephani aram Deo*"[129]. Of the early Sacramentaries, the Gelasian Sacramentary has a reference in the Mass of Dedication to the relics of the saints in the Altar. We see the mentioning of relics in *GeV* No. 692, "*Mitus enim ponis super cornu Altaris digito tuo vinum cum aqua mixtum; et asperges Altare septem vicibus, reliquum autem fundes ad basem. Et offeris incensum super Altare odorem suauissimum domino*"[130]. In the history we can see that the Eucharist was also celebrated in the burial place of the dead and even in the prisons of those held captives[131].

The first step toward a revision of the legislation concerning relics came with promulgation of the Roman Missal by Paul VI on April 3, 1969. The General Instruction, in fact, attenuates the obligation to use a sacred stone: Regarding the depositing of the relics, the Instruction No. 266 said, "*Usus includenti in Altari consecrando, vel deponendi sub Altari, reliquas Sanctorum, etsi non Martyrum, opportune servetur.*

---

[126] AMBROSIUS, «De Corporum Inventione SS. Martyrum Protasi et Gervasi Sermones Duo :Epistola XXII, ad Marcellinam», in *Sancti Ambrosii Mediolanensis Episcopi, ecclesiae patris ac doctoris Opera Omnia ad mediolanenses codices pressius exacta*, ed. P. A. Ballerini, Typographia Sancti Josephi, Mediolani 1881, 157-164,161.

[127] *Ordo Dedicationis Ecclesiae et Altaris, Pontificale Romanum, Ex Decreto Sacrosancti Ecumenici Concili Vaticani II Instauratum Auctoritate Pauli PP. VI Promulgatum*, 84.

[128] *The Roman Pontifical Revised by Decree of the Second Vatican Ecumenical Council and Published by Authority of Pope Paul VI. Dedication of a Church and an Altar*, tr. International Committee on English in the Liturgy, United States Catholic Conference, Inc., Washington 1989, 66. (Hereafter cited as *Dedication of a Church and an Altar*).

[129] AUGUSTINUS, «Sermo CCCXVIII: De Martyre Stephano V», in *Collectio selecta SS. Ecclesiae Patrum complectens Exquitissima opera tum Dogmatica et Moralia, tum Apologetica et Oratoria: Sancti Aurelii Augustini Hipponensis Episcopi Operum Pars IV. Opera Oratoria*, ed. D. A. Caillau, Parent-Desbarres, Paris 1838, 142-146, 144.

[130] *Liber Sacramentorum Romanæ Æclesiæ ordinis anni circuli* (Cod. Vat. Reg. lat. 316/Paris Bibl. Nat. 7193, 41/56) (*Sacramentarium Gelasianum*), ed. L. Eizenhofer-P. Siffrin-L. C. Mohlberg-(Rerum Ecclesiasticarum Documenta Series Maior, Fontes 4), Herder, Roma 1981, 108.

[131] J. JUNGMANN, *The Mass of the Roman Rite: Its Origin and Development Vol I*, 253.

*Caveatur tame nut de huiusmodi reliquiarum veritate certo consetet*"[132]. By saying this, the Church affirms the practice of enclosing relics in the Altar or of placing them under the Altar. These relics need not be those of martyrs, but there must be proof that they are authentic. The Rite of Dedication of a Church and an Altar No. 60, with delicate precision, points out:

> Qui versus sacerdos veraque effectus hostia, sacrificii, quod ipse in ara crucis tibi obtulit, memorial nobis praecepit in perpetuum celebrare. Ideo Populus tuus hoc erexit Altare, quod tibi, Domine, exsultantes dicamus. Hic est vere locus excelsus, ubi Christi sacrificium in mysterio iugiter offertur, tibi perfecta tribuitur laus nostraque exseritur redemptio....[133]

Although all the saints are rightly called Christ's witnesses, the witness of blood has a special significance, which is given complete and perfect expression by depositing only martyrs' relics beneath the Altar[134].

The act of depositing of relics, the revised rite proposes singing Psalm 14, introduced by one of the two antiphons: 'The bodies of the saints lie buried in peace, but their names will live forever (alleluia)' or 'Saints of God, you have been enthroned at the foot of God's Altar; pray for us to the Lord Jesus Christ'[135]. The choice of Psalm 14, was probably dictated by the meaning of the *depositio*: the resting place of mortal remains in a dwelling place of holiness and peace, the Eucharistic Altar. As well, it is a sign of the martyrs' entry, following upon a heroic following of Christ, into the 'tent' of the Lord, their resting place on the holy mountain where they will enjoy eternal rest[136].

Lumen Gentium 50, "*Apostolos autem et martyres Christi, qui sui sanguinis effusione supremum fidei et caritatis testimonium dederant, in Christo arctius nobis*

---

[132] *Institutio Generalis Missalis Romani No. 266*, in Missale Romanum Ex Decreto Sacrosancti Oecumenici Concilii Vaticani II, Instauratum auctoritate Pauli PP.VI promulgatum, Ordo Missae, Typis Polyglottis Vaticanis, Romae 1969, 62.

[133] *Ordo Dedicationis Ecclesiae et Altaris, Pontificale Romanum, Ex Decreto Sacrosancti Ecumenici Concili Vaticani II Instauratum Auctoritate Pauli PP. VI Promulgatum*, 108-109. tr. "True priest and true victim, he offered himself to you on the Altar of the cross and commanded us to celebrate that same sacrifice, until he comes again. Therefore your people have built this Altar and have dedicated it to your name with grateful hearts. This is a truly sacred place. Here the sacrifice of Christ is offered in mystery, perfect praise is given to you, and our redemption is made continually present". Quoted from *Dedication of a Church and an Altar*, 85.

[134] M. C. IGNAZIO, *The Dedication of a Church and an Altar: A Theological Commentary*, 22.

[135] *Ordo Dedicationis Ecclesiae et Altaris, Pontificale Romanum, Ex Decreto Sacrosancti Ecumenici Concili Vaticani II Instauratum Auctoritate Pauli PP. VI Promulgatum*, 109.

[136] M. C. IGNAZIO, *The Dedication of a Church and an Altar: A Theological Commentary*, 20-23.

*coniunctos esse Ecclesia semper credidit...*"[137]. Both martyrs and saints are friends and co-heirs of Jesus Christ, and also brothers and outstanding benefactors of the faithful. Built of Living Stones, No. 60 says that in the Church's history and tradition, the Altar was often placed over the tombs of the saints or the relics of saints were deposited beneath the Altar. The presence of the relics of saints in the Altar provides a witness to the Church's belief that the Eucharist celebrated on the Altar is the source of the grace that won sanctity for the saints[138]. Code of Canon Law, Can. 1237 § 2 says, "*Antiqua traditio Martyrum aliorumve Sanctorum reliquias sub Altari fixo condendi servetur, iuxta normas in libris liturgicis traditas*"[139].

As the Eucharist is a joining of the Church in Christ's sacrifice, it can be expressed in the body of a holy man or woman who exhibited that sacrifice in their life. That is, the body or relic of the saint is a material reminder of Christ's one immemorial sacrifice and bodily death[140]. The deposition of relics has the further motive of associating with that of the saints, whenever the believers come together in the church to pray[141].

CONCLUSION TO THE FIRST CHAPTER

From the beginning, the Christians differentiated their Altars from pagan ones even by the usage of the terms. In the Bible, the evolution of the idea of Altar grew gradually. The Altar was a symbol of God's presence and the gifts placed on the Altar was sanctified merely by contact with the Altar. The sacrifice was offered on the Altar and it became the table to offer food for God and people ate that which was offered to God believing that it was sanctified and given back by God Himself to have communion

---

[137] CONCILIUM OECUMENICUM VATICANUM II, Constitutio Dogmatica de Ecclesia *Lumen Gentium 50*, *AAS* 57 (1965) 5-71, 55. tr. "The Church has always believed that the apostles and Christ's martyrs who had given the supreme witness of faith and charity by the shedding of their blood, are closely joined with us in Christ, and she has always venerated them with special devotion…". Quoted from VATICAN COUNCIL II, *Lumen Gentium*: in *The Conciliar and Post Conciliar Documents* 1, 411.
[138] UNITED STATES CONFERENCE OF CATHOLIC BISHOPS, *Built of Living Stones: Art, Architecture, and Worship*, 24.
[139] *Code of Canon Law Annotated*, 765. tr. "The ancient tradition of placing relics of Martrys or of other Saints beneath a fixed Altar is to be retained, in accordance with the rites prescribed in the liturgical books". Quoted from *Code of Canon Law Annotated*, 765.
[140] M. C. IGNAZIO, *The Dedication of a Church and an Altar: A Theological Commentary*, 23.
[141] L. CHENGALIKAVIL, *The Mystery of Christ and the Church in the Dedication of a Church*, Pontificium Athenaeum Anselmianum, Rome 1984, 37.

with them. In the sacrifice, also vegetables, products of vegetables and incense were gradually offered. In the New Testament, Jesus perpetuated his Cross Sacrifice in the Sacramental forms of bread and wine in his Last Supper. Therefore, the table became the Altar and the sacrifice is done in sacramental forms. Thereafter, the Altar became essential in the Christian worship.

As the image of the rock is connected with Christ, He is seen as the unique Altar in the apostolic period. In some of the pagan religions, we also see the usage of the Altar. There the Altar serves as a base for the sacrifice which is offered to appease God or to have communion with God. Moreover, these sacrifices are only man's inventions. However, the Catholic Altar is unique and special, because the sacrifice is not manmade but Christ Himself is the priest, the Altar and the victim. In the history of the Christian Altar, one can see many interpretations given to the Altar and the practice of embellishment made the Altar surrounded and vested with many elements which obscured the true nature of Altar. Gradually, the Church affirmed the true nature of the Altar and the necessity to remove those elements that obscure its true character. In the patristic period, one can relish the wonderful theological connotations evolving about the Altar. Meanwhile, the Church documents give clear vision of the Altar in the liturgical celebrations and directions to keep the Altar holy.

As the Altar is the central feature and the focal point of the church, one should also know its connection with the tabernacle, relics and its orientation. Though the tabernacle is one of the important elements in a church, the Altar is the center of the Liturgical Worship. In the question of orientation, the Church gives a clear indication to build the Altar separate from the wall, free standing and advocates Eucharistic celebration facing the people. The practice of keeping the relics of the saints or the martyrs under the altar goes back to the earlier centuries and brings out the sacrificial aspect of the Altar. It emphasizes that the Eucharist celebrated on the altar is the source of grace for those saints and martyrs.

**Altar at one of the oldest churches in Trent, Italy where the Council of Trent was held**

# CHAPTER TWO
# UNDERSTANDING GESTURES, VENERATION AND SYMBOLISM WITH REGARD TO THE ALTAR

The United States Conference of Catholic Bishops, in the document *Built of Living Stones number 23,* says that the gestures, languages, and actions are the physical, visible, and public expressions by which human beings understand and manifest their life. Since human beings on this earth are always made of flesh and blood, they not only will and think, but also speak and sing, move and celebrate[142]. These human actions as well as physical objects are also the signs by which Christians express and deepen their relationship to God.

In explaining the Sacraments of Initiation, St. Ambrose writes that the baptized Christian sees the Altar with the eyes of Faith. *De Sacramentis III, 11, "Venire habes ad Altare. Quoniam venisti videre habes quae ante non videbas..."*[143]. Therefore, by seeing or realizing what happens on the Altar, one comes to know many theological elements involved in the Eucharistic celebration. Guardini says that man searches in the liturgy, consciously or not, the epiphany, the bright appearance of the sacred reality in the liturgy; the sound appearance of the Eternal Word in speech and song; the presence of the Holy Spirit in the corporeity of tangible things[144]. Therefore, we should try to analyze the symbols and gestures involved in the liturgy. In this chapter I will try to explore some of the gestures, veneration and symbolism with regard to the Altar.

## 2.1. GESTURES AND VENERATION CENTERED AROUND THE ALTAR

The Most Holy object in a church is the Altar, which is also the focus of the mass, and deserves the greatest attention and veneration[145]. According to the mind of the Church an Altar is primarily the stone of sacrifice on which the divine Victim is

---

[142] UNITED STATES CONFERENCE OF CATHOLIC BISHOPS, *Built of Living Stones: Art, Architecture, and Worship*, 23.
[143] AMBROSIUS, «De Sacramentis», in *Des Sacraments Des Mysteres*, ed. D.B. Botte, (Sources Chrétiennes 25), Paris 1949, 75.
[144] R. GUARDINI, «La funzione della sensibilità nella conoscenza religiosa», in *Scritti filosofici vol II*, Fabbri, Milano 1964, 135-190, 164.
[145] G. S. DUNCAN, *The Church Building as a Sacred Place: Beauty, Transcendence, and the Eternal*, 20.

offered; it is also the sacred table from which the people are fed with the Body of Christ, and a tomb in which the relics of his martyrs lie buried.

> The Altar is a holy place by:
> (1) its solemn consecration, by an elaborate rite of lustrations, anointings, incensings, with numerous prayers, etc., whereby it is, as it were, baptized, confirmed and hallowed for its sacred purpose;
> (2) its use as the stone of sacrifice and the table of the Divine Banquet;
> (3) its symbolism as the figure of Christ (the anointed King, Priest and Prophet), of Calvary and of the Table of the Last Supper[146].

Therefore, this holy place is venerated by means of gestures and adornment. Jungmann says that in the Gothic period, the Mass is looked upon as a holy drama, a play performed before the eyes of the participants. Meanwhile the graphic ceremonial has been enriched. The sign of the cross, kissing the Altar, extension of hands and bowing are the few ceremonies[147].

Pope John Paul II, in his Apostolic Letter *Vicesimus Quintus Annus*, on the 25th Anniversary of the Promulgation of the Conciliar Constitution *Sacrosanctum Concilium* on the Sacred Liturgy in article 7, says as follows,

> In hanc Domini praesentiam fides secum infert externum erga Ecclesiam observantiae signum, locum nempe sacrum ubi suo se in mysterio Deus demonstrat (Ex 3, 5), praesertim cum sacramenta celebrantur: semper enim sunt sancte sancta tractanda[148].

The United States Conference of Catholic Bishops, in the document *Built of Living Stones number 25*, says that to the central signs, the Church adds gestures and material elements such as incense, holy water, candles, and vestments to dispose us for the heavenly gifts of our Risen Lord and to deepen our reverence for the unceasing mercy and grace that come to us in the Church through the passion and death of Jesus, our Lord[149]. Gestures and symbols lead us to the grace and mercy of God.

---

[146] J. B. O'CONNELL, *Church Building and Furnishing*, 161.
[147] J. JUNGMANN, *The Mass of the Roman Rite: Its Origin and Development Vol I*, 107.
[148] JOHN PAUL II, *Vicesimus Quintus Annus, Quinto iam lustro expleto conciliari ab promulgata de Sacra Liturgia Constitutione Sacrosanctum Concilium, AAS 81* (1989) 904. tr. "Faith in this presence of the Lord involves an outward sign of respect towards the Church, the holy place in which God manifests himself in mystery (see Ex 3, 5), especially during the celebration of the sacraments: holy things must always be treated in a holy manner". Quoted from G. S. Duncan, *The Church Building as a Sacred Place: Beauty, Transcendence, and the Eternal*, 20.
[149] UNITED STATES CONFERENCE OF CATHOLIC BISHOPS, *Built of Living Stones (2000)*, 426.

J. B. O'Connell says in his book 'Church Building and Furnishing' that due respect is being given to the Altar by various means.

> Accordingly, the Church honors the high Altar as the sacred place in the church: the ministers of the sanctuary bow or genuflect to it; the celebrant kisses it no less than eight times in the course of a solemn Mass, and he alone may place his hands on its table when he genuflects there; it is incensed at High Mass, at Lauds and Vespers; lights burn before it; on Maundy Thursday, after *Tenebrae*, it is washed with wine and water by the Bishop and his clergy in some cathedrals. Because, then, of the sanctity of the high Altar the Church orders that it be specially honored by being surmounted by a canopy and clothed with a frontal and Altar cloths, and permits that it be adorned, on occasion, with reliquaries and flowers. Because of its consecration, its symbolism and its use, the Altar is to be austere dignified, majestic and awesome. This sacred character of the Altar is emphasized and secured from disrespect when the laws of the Church concerning its structure and ornamentation are observed[150].

The ritual elements, especially gestures, were to express a decidedly Christological and Ecclesial content[151]. *Sacrosanctum Concilium* when describing the gestures in the Liturgy laid down the following principle covering the reform of gestures:

> Ritus nobili simplicitate fulgeant, sint breavitate perspicui et repetitions inutiles evident, sint fidelium captui accomodati, neque generatim multis indegeant explanationibus[152].

In this chapter, the gestures and veneration around the holy Altar and their historical and theological background, along with the symbolism of the Altar, are dealt with.

## 2.1.1. INCENSING THE ALTAR

In the use of incense in the religious context, we can try to understand the Old Testament understanding of incense. Of the first Altar Scripture says: "Noah built an Altar to the Lord ... he offered holocausts on the Altar ... the Lord smelled the sweet odour" (Gen 8, 20-21). At a very early time, incense, because of its fragrant spirals, became the symbol of that sacrifice performed on the Altar: the rising to God in an

---

[150] J. B. O'CONNELL, *Church Building and Furnishing*, 161.
[151] M. C. IGNAZIO, *The Dedication of a Church and an Altar: A Theological Commentary*, 29.
[152] CONCILIUM OECUMENICUM VATICANUM II, Constitutio de Sacra Liturgia *Sacrosanctum Concilium 34*, 109. tr. "The rites should be distinguished by a noble simplicity; they should be short, clear, and unencumbered by useless repetition; they should be within the people's power of comprehension and as rule not require much explanation". Quoted from VATICAN COUNCIL II, *Sacrosanctum Concilium*, 12.

acceptable way. Israel, in organizing its worship, used incense as the ritual scent frequently and abundantly[153].

According to an anthropomorphic Old Testament conception YHWH takes pleasure in inhaling the soothing odour (*rêah hannîhoah*) of offerings (Gen 8, 21; Ex 29, 18; 1 Sam 26, 19 and also Lev 26, 31; Amos 5, 21)[154]. Wherever sweet-smelling odours spread, life is flourishing and health and vitality are made manifest (Hos 8, 17; Song of Solomon 6, 11)[155]. Incense of the prescribed composition is reserved by YHWH for himself. By claiming the exclusive right to the blend of the holy incense, YHWH reserves its special fragrance for himself. Therefore, the odour becomes an expression of his personality[156]. Offering incense to YHWH without interruption is one of the conditions on which YHWH will be present at the sanctuary. When YHWH is present, His special fragrance should be felt in the sanctuary[157].

YHWH desires to inhale (Deut 33, 10) only pure fragrance. This anthropomorphic concept is the basis for the idea that the time of the incense-offering is the best time for prayer (Luke 1, 10-11). The words of the prayer mingle as it were with the rising fragrant smoke (Ps 141, 1-2; Rev 5, 8; 8, 3-4). God inhales it, enjoys it and so in an excellent mood he absorbs as it were at the same time the words of the prayer. So the prayer stands a good chance of meeting a favorable response[158].

The Old Testament idea of incense also has its effect on the New Testament conception and practice of the usage of incense. Christ's self-giving functioned as the sweet smelling offerings of the Old Testament tradition[159]. The fragrance acceptable to the Father is that which comes from Christ's Easter sacrifice, as we read in St. Paul: "Follow the way of love, even as Christ loved you. He gave himself for us as an offering to God, a gift of pleasing fragrance" (Eph 5, 2). The Book of Revelation (5, 8;

---

[153] M. C. IGNAZIO, *The Dedication of a Church and an Altar: A Theological Commentary*, 29.

[154] H. CORNELIS, «On the function of the holy incense (Exodus 30:34-8) and the sacred anointing oil (Exodus 30:22-33)», in *Vetus Testamentum 42* (1992/4) 458.

[155] H. CORNELIS, «On the function of the holy incense (Exodus 30:34-8) and the sacred anointing oil (Exodus 30:22-33)», 459.

[156] H. CORNELIS, «On the function of the holy incense (Exodus 30:34-8) and the sacred anointing oil (Exodus 30:22-33)», 462.

[157] H. CORNELIS, «On the function of the holy incense (Exodus 30:34-8) and the sacred anointing oil (Exodus 30:22-33)», 463.

[158] H. CORNELIS, «On the function of the holy incense (Exodus 30:34-8) and the sacred anointing oil (Exodus 30:22-33)», 464.

[159] T. B. BOWMAN, «2 Corinthians 2:14-16a: Christ's incense», in *Restoration Quarterly 29* (1987/2) 68.

8, 3-4) says that incense, besides symbolizing the 'acceptable fragrance', is also a symbol of prayer that rises to God[160].

During the consecration of the Altar, on five points of the Altar signed with holy chrism there burned five crosses made of wax and grains of incense. The Altar became a field of fire from which arose dense clouds of smoke and fragrant balsam[161]. Added to that, in the consecration rite, the bishop envelopes the Altar in the perfumed clouds of smoke, the prayers of the saints, as the book of Revelation tells us, rising before the eternal throne[162].

St. Ambrose in his work, *De Sacramentis* in Catechesis Four, Chapter I. 4, writes that every Christian is a sweet odour like Christ.

> In secundo quoque tabernaculo est thymiamaterium. Thymiamaterium est quod bonum odorem fragrare consueuit. Ita et vos iam bonus odor Christi estis, iam nulla in vobis sors delicatorum, nullus odor grauioris erroris[163].

Jungmann when he explains the historical development adds that the incensation at the offertory is therefore a fruit of Carolingian liturgical development. In particular, the incensing at the offertory became far more prominent than the incensations at the beginning of Mass and at the Gospel. This prominence has been retained in our current liturgy, as is seen in the fact that it is richest in prayers[164].

In *De Antiquitas Ecclesiae Ritibus. Lib. I. Cap. IV. Art. XII*, we see prayers accompanied with incensing. After *Per intercessionem beati Gabrielis archangeli* we see a prayer for incensing the bread and the Chalice:

> Memores sumus aeterne Deus, Pater omnipotens, glorisissimae passionis Filii tui, resurrectionis etiam ejus, et ascensionis ejus in coelum. Petimus ergo Majestatem tuam, ut ascendant preces humilitatis nostrae una cum incense isto in conspectum tuae clementiae, et descendat super hunc panem et super hunc calicem plenitude Divinitatis. Descendat etiam Domine illa

---

[160] M. C. IGNAZIO, *The Dedication of a Church and an Altar: A Theological Commentary*, 29.
[161] M. C. IGNAZIO, *The Dedication of a Church and an Altar: A Theological Commentary*, 29.
[162] E. MCDONALD, «The Consecration of the Altar», in *Orate Fratres 6* (1932/8) 359-365, 360.
[163] AMBROSIUS, «De Sacramentis », in *Des Sacraments Des Mysteres*, ed. D.B. Botte (Sources Chrétiennes 25), Paris 1949, 53-107, 79. tr. "the inner tabernacle also contains the Altar of incense, which customarily burns with good odour. And so you also are the sweet fragrance of Christ; no stain of sin is in you, no odour of serious error". Quoted from AMBROSE, «De Sacramentis (on the Sacraments)» , in *Worship in the Early Church: An Anthology of Historical Sources Vol 2*, ed. & tr. L. J. Johnson, Liturgical Press, Minnesota 2009, 40-69, 54.
[164] J. JUNGMANN, *The Mass of the Roman Rite: Its Origin and Development Vol II*, 71.

>Sancti Spiritus incomprehensibilis invisibilisque majestas, sicut quondam in Patrum hostias descendebat...[165]

We thus meet here, for the first time, a prayer for the moment the incense is being put into the censer: "*Per intercessionem beati Gabrielis archangeli*", with a petition to bless the incense and to receive it 'for a sweet savor'.

In the *Missale Romanum* after the Council of Trent, we see a further prayer accompanying the incensation: "*Incensum istud, a te benedictum, ascendat ad te, Domine: et descendat super nos misericordia tua*"[166]. This prayer is continued with the Psalm 140, 2-4: "*Dirigatur oratio mea sicut incensum in conspectu tuo, Domine.....*"[167]. Finally, there is a formula spoken by the celebrant when he puts the censer back into the hands of the deacon: "*Accendat in nobis Dominus ignem sui amoris et flammam aeternae caritatis*"[168].

Maggiani calls it as an 'olfactory code' and says that it always produces reactions in anyone to whom it is directed. Incense has the ability to evoke, call and provoke[169]. The only thing asked for is that the incense might ascend to God and God's mercy might descend to us. These words give us a clue to the meaning then attributed to this incensation, significance similar to what we saw on earlier occasions: the incense is something dedicated to God, something holy, in which, by a sort of communion, we want to be associated. The glowing coal and the smoke arising from it draw the mind to the very highest thing that we can beg of God as answer to our offerings, the fire of divine love[170].

We can symbolize our abasement before God both by word and by signs, even by gifts of our own selection, and there are no gifts as expressive as the incense which is consumed in the charcoal, and then rises skyward in fragrant clouds. The incensing of

---

[165] *De Antiquis Ecclesiae Ritibus Libri: Ex variis insigniorum Ecclesiarum Pontificalibus, Sacramentariis, Missalibus, Breviariis, Ritualibus, seu Manualibus, Ordinariis seu Consuetudinariis, cum manuscriptis tum editis; ex diversis Conciliorum Decretis, Episcoporum Statutis, aliisque probatis Auctoribus permultis*, ed. E. Martene, Antuerpiae, Typis Joannis Baptistae de la Bry 1736, 511.
[166] *Ordo Missae*, in *Missale Romanum Ex Decreto Sacrosancti Concilii Tridentini Restitutum Summorum Pontificum Cura Recognitum*, Editio Prima Iuxta Typicam, Sumptibus et Typis Mame, Romae 1962, 312.
[167] *Ordo Missae*, 312.
[168] *Ordo Missae*, 312.
[169] S. MAGGIANI, «The Language of Liturgy», in *Liturgical Science* II, ed. A. J, Chupungco, A Pueblo Book, Minnesota 227-255, 254.
[170] J. JUNGMANN, *The Mass of the Roman Rite: Its Origin and Development Vol II*, 70-71.

the Altar and the congregation, is intended to envelop the gifts in the holy atmosphere of prayer which ascend to God like an incense cloud; thus it is intended to symbolically represent and to fortify the primary action at the Altar[171].

In *Ordo Dedicationis Ecclesiae et Altaris* we see the following prayer which calls all the Christians to be the fragrance of Christ in the world we live.

> Dirigatur, Domine, oratio nostra
> Sicut incensum in conspectus tuo
> Et sicut haec domus suavi repletur odore
> Ita Ecclesia tua redoleat Christi fragrantiam[172].

St. Paul says, "We are indeed the incense offered by Christ to God" (2Cor 2, 15). Paul uses the language of sacrifice in which fragrance ascends to God and engenders a favourable attitude towards humanity. We have a theological implication that the Christians are the incense or perfume; its essence is Christ[173]. Ceremonial of Bishops, numbers 84-98 speak about the incensation in various celebrations.

> The rite of incensation or thurification is a sign of reverence and of prayer, as is clear from Psalm 141: 2 and Revelation 8: 3 (No.84).
> The substance placed in the censer should be pure sweet-scented incense or at least in larger proportion than any additive mixed with the incense (No.85).
> At the stational Mass of the bishop incense should be used: at the beginning of Mass to incense the Altar and at the presentation of the gifts, to incense the gifts, the Altar, the cross, the bishop, the concelebrants, and the people (No.86).
> At the solemn celebration of morning or evening prayer the Altar, the bishop, and the people may be incensed during the singing of the Gospel canticle (No.89).
> The Altar is incensed with a series of single swings of the censer (No.93)[174].

Having understood the usage of Incense, we try to deepen our comprehension from the view point of Guardini. He writes in his book 'Sacred Signs', the meaning and the theology behind the incensation:

---

[171] J. JUNGMANN, *The Mass of the Roman Rite: Its Origin and Development Vol II*, 72-76.
[172] *Ordo Dedicationis Ecclesiae et Altaris, Pontificale Romanum, Ex Decreto Sacrosancti Ecumenici Concili Vaticani II Instauratum Auctoritate Pauli PP. VI Promulgatum*, 50. tr. "Lord, may our prayer ascend as incense in your sight. As this building is filled with fragrance so may your Church fill the world with the fragrance of Christ". Quoted from *Dedication of a Church and an Altar*, 56.
[173] T. B. BOWMAN, «2 Corinthians 2:14-16a: Christ's incense», 67.
[174] INTERNATIONAL COMMISSION ON ENGLISH IN THE LITURGY, *Ceremonial of Bishops: Revised by Decree of the Second Vatican Ecumenical Council and Published by Authority of Pope John Paul II*, 40-41.

> The offering of an incense is a generous and beautiful rite. The bright grains of incense are laid upon the red-hot charcoal, the censer is swung, and the fragrant smoke rises in clouds. In the rhythm and the sweetness there is a musical quality; and like music also is the entire lack of practical utility: it is a prodigal waste of precious material. It is a pouring out of unwithholding love[175].

Guardini quotes the incident of Mary anointing the feet of Jesus with the precious perfume (Mt 26, 3-9; Jn 12, 1-8). Mary's anointing was a mystery of death and love and the sweet savour of sacrifice. The offering of incense is like Mary's anointing at Bethany. It is as free and objectless as beauty. It burns and is consumed like love that lasts through death[176].

> Incense is the symbol of prayer. Like pure prayer it has in view no object of its own; it asks nothing for itself. Prayer is not to be measured by its bargaining power; it is not a matter of bourgeois common sense. Minds of this order know nothing of that magnanimous prayer that seeks only to give. Prayer is a profound act of worship, that asks neither why nor wherefore. It rises like beauty, like sweetness, like love. The more there is in it of love, the more of sacrifice. And when the fire has wholly consumed the sacrifice, a sweet savour ascends[177].

Thus, Incensing is a symbol of prayers ascending to God and every Christian is called to be like that incense with the fragrance of Christ.

## 2.1.2. KISSING THE ALTAR

The most frequent and most unmistakable sign of love is the kiss. Kissing the Altar has a greater significance in the Liturgy. In the Roman Stational services in the 7th century, after the '*Gloria Patri*' and the prostration, the Pope, after a moment, rises, kisses the Gospel book and the Altar. Meanwhile, during the interval of silent prayer, the deacons have come up to the sides of the Altar two-by-two and kissed it[178]. In the same liturgy, after the offertory, the Pontiff leaves his place and kisses the Altar and then he receives the oblation of the assisting clerics[179].

Jungmann, when explaining the historical development of the gesture of kissing the Altar, says:

---

[175] R. GUARDINI, *Sacred Signs*, tr. G. Branham, Pio Decimo Press, Missouri 1956, 28.
[176] R. GUARDINI, *Sacred Signs*, 28-29.
[177] R. GUARDINI, *Sacred Signs*, 29.
[178] J. JUNGMANN, *The Mass of the Roman Rite: Its Origin and Development Vol I*, 70.
[179] J. JUNGMANN, *The Mass of the Roman Rite: Its Origin and Development Vol I*, 71.

The Gothic principle of cumulation, the heaping up of ornament, had its effect on the kissing of the Altar. Although up to the twelfth century, this was customary, in line with tradition, only when first approaching the Altar and again when leaving, since the end of the thirteenth century it was performed every time the celebrant turned around at the Altar. The kiss at high Mass when handing the celebrant any object, and the kiss of greeting for the celebrant are also added at various places[180].

No less than eight times in the Tridentine Mass, the officiating priest bends low to kiss the Altar (*Osculatur Altare*)[181]. However, in the revised *Ordo* after Vatican II, we see the priest kisses the Altar only two times. When the priest approaches the Altar for the Eucharistic celebration and when he leaves the Altar after the mass, kisses the Altar accompanied with a deep bow as a sign of veneration[182]:

> Cum ad presbyterium pervenerint, sacerdos, diaconus, et ministri Altare salutant *profunda inclinatione*. Venerationis autem significandæ causa, sacerdos et diaconus ipsum Altare deinde *osculantur*; et sacerdos, pro opportunitate, crucem et Altare incensat[183]. Ad ritus conclusionis pertinent: d) *osculatio Altaris* ex parte sacerdotis et diaconi et deinde *inclinatio profunda* ad Altare ex parte sacerdotis, diaconi, aliorumque ministrorum[184].

The book of ceremonies says that the ceremonial kiss is a very ancient sign of respect and reverence and the Altar is kissed because it represents Christ[185]. In the General Instruction, there is also a special instruction about the veneration of the Altar and the book of the Gospels. *De veneratione Altaris et Evangeliarii number 273, "Iuxta morem traditum, veneratio Altaris et Evangeliarii osculo perficitur..."*[186]. The book of

---

[180] J. JUNGMANN, *The Mass of the Roman Rite: Its Origin and Development Vol I*, 107.
[181] Ordo Missae, in *Missale Romanum Ex Decreto Sacrosancti Tridentini Restitutum Summorum Pontificum Cura Recognitum*, Editio Prima Iuxta Typicam, Sumptibus et Typis Mame, Romae-Turonibus-Parisiis 1969, 308, 310, 311, 313, 397, 404-405, 411 and 415.
[182] *Institutio Generalis Missalis Romani No. 49, 90, 123, 169, 173, 211, 251 & 256*, in *Missale Romanum Ex Decreto Sacrosancti Oecumenici Concilii Vaticani II, Instauratum auctoritate Pauli PP.VI promulgatum Ioannis Pauli PP. II cura recognitum*, 30, 39, 46, 51, 52, 56 & 61.
[183] *Institutio Generalis Missalis Romani No. 49*, in *Missale Romanum Ex Decreto Sacrosancti Oecumenici Concilii Vaticani II, Instauratum auctoritate Pauli PP.VI promulgatum Ioannis Pauli PP. II cura recognitum*, 30.
[184] *Institutio Generalis Missalis Romani No. 90d*, in *Missale Romanum Ex Decreto Sacrosancti Oecumenici Concilii Vaticani II, Instauratum auctoritate Pauli PP.VI promulgatum Ioannis Pauli PP. II cura recognitum*, 39.
[185] L. J. O'CONNELL, *The Book of ceremonies*, The Bruce Publishing company, Wisconsin 1943, 40.
[186] *Institutio Generalis Missalis Romani No. 273*, in *Missale Romanum Ex Decreto Sacrosancti Oecumenici Concilii Vaticani II, Instauratum auctoritate Pauli PP.VI promulgatum Ioannis Pauli PP. II cura recognitum*, 63.

the Ceremonial of Bishops, number 73 also discusses about this sign of veneration of kissing the Altar[187].

In *Ordo Dedicationis Ecclesiae et Altaris*, number 35 we see, "*Episcopus, omisso Altaris osculo, pergit ad cathedram*"[188]. The omission of the gesture of kissing the Altar, which is completely stripped, is understandable since this sign of veneration is given only after the Altar has been anointed with chrism[189]. The kiss of the Altar with which every Eucharistic celebration begins had been deferred because the Altar was not ready. And after the consecration, now the Altar, having become the sign of the Anointed One and decorated as a joyous Easter table, is ready to receive the ritual gesture of veneration with which every Eucharist begins and ends[190].

The Eastern Father Narsai of Nisibus (ca. 399-503), write in his 'Homilies' about the Eucharistic sacrifice, in which he describes the veneration of Altar by the priests:

> The priest stands to officiate, doing so with reverence, great awe, and trembling. Like Jacob, he worships three times and three; then he draws near to kiss our Lord's tomb, that is, Altar[191].

Bradley sees it is a brotherly greeting. Taking the idea of St. Paul in 1Thes 5, 26: 'Greet one another with a holy kiss', he says that the concept of the Altar as Christ's body is expressed by the priest's kissing it, particularly as an act of brotherly greeting at the beginning of Mass[192]. Behen gives a different understanding from the idea of Bradley. He says that although the kiss seems to be a sign of veneration for the relics enclosed in the Altar, we must see a deeper significance in the gesture than that. The frequent repetition of the act reminds us of the bridal relation between Christ that is the Altar and His Church that is the priest, the representative of the Church. Especially significant is the kiss of peace immediately preceding the sacrificial banquet. The kiss,

---

[187] INTERNATIONAL COMMISSION ON ENGLISH IN THE LITURGY, *Ceremonial of Bishops: Revised by Decree of the Second Vatican Ecumenical Council and Published by Authority of Pope John Paul II*, 37.
[188] *Ordo Dedicationis Ecclesiae et Altaris, Pontificale Romanum, Ex Decreto Sacrosancti Ecumenici Concili Vaticani II Instauratum Auctoritate Pauli PP. VI Promulgatum*, 34.
[189] M. C. IGNAZIO, *The Dedication of a Church and an Altar: A Theological Commentary*, 12.
[190] M. C. IGNAZIO, *The Dedication of a Church and an Altar: A Theological Commentary*, 34.
[191] NARSAI OF NISIBUS, «Homilies», 291.
[192] J. P. BRADLEY, *The Catholic Layman's Library Vol 3*, 392.

symbolizing the Christian love of the assembled faithful, proceeds from the Altar. The celebrant first kisses the Altar which is Christ and then kisses his brethren[193].

Bradley sees it as brotherly greetings while Behen sees the same as the bridal kiss of the Church through the priest to the groom Jesus symbolized in the Altar. The Kiss involves the senses of touch, taste, and smell[194]. Therefore, it's an expression of close relationship. The kiss communicates affection and it also involves sharing[195]. In explaining the kiss of peace, L. E. Philips says that the kiss could also function as a communication of Spiritual power and or other qualities contained within *Pneuma*[196]. The giving of the Holy Spirit in the Gospel of John 20:22, is interpreted very much like a kiss[197]. Therefore, the kiss of a priest can also be thought of in this view point. After receiving the Spiritual power from Jesus at the Altar, the priest exercises his priestly ministry at the Altar.

## 2.1.3. BOWING AND GENUFLECTING BEFORE THE ALTAR

Both bowing and genuflecting are signs of veneration and reverence. Bowing is a gesture of showing one's humbleness. Especially, when one bows before God, he surrenders himself to the will of God.

Caesarius of Arles (ca. 470-542), in his sermon 'an admonition to kneel for prayer and to bow at the blessing', writes:

> My brothers and sisters, I ask that as often as you pray at the Altar you bow your heads. Doing so, you will avoid what was written about the Pharisee (Lk 18, 10-14) who, standing erect, praised his own merits[198].

Behen say that the Christian Altar is also the throne of God. Here on the Altar of Christ, the divine King becomes present on earth through the Eucharistic Sacrifice. The Altar has always been considered the throne of Christ. Therefore, we have another reason for saying, 'The Altar is Christ', for the throne symbolizes the person of the

---

[193] M. J. BEHEN, «The Christian Altar», 427.
[194] L. E. PHILIPS, *The Ritual Kiss in Early Christian Worship*, Groove Books Limited, Cambridge 1996, 5.
[195] L. E. PHILIPS, *The Ritual Kiss in Early Christian Worship*, 5.
[196] L. E. PHILIPS, *The Ritual Kiss in Early Christian Worship*, 5.
[197] L. E. PHILIPS, *The Ritual Kiss in Early Christian Worship*, 13-14.
[198] CAESARIUS, «Sermon 76: An admonition to kneel for prayer and to bow at the blessing», in *Worship in the Early Church: An Anthology of Historical Sources Vol 4*, ed. & tr. L. J. Johnson, Liturgical Press, Minnesota 2009, 106-107, 107.

ruler. The Christian ought to approach the Altar-throne with a more profound reverence than the Jewish high priest approached the Holy of holies[199].

Behen tries to explain the importance of the veneration of the Altar taking the Eastern Church practices. The aspect of reverence to the Altar is more clearly expressed in the Eastern Church.

> The most characteristic feature of the Eastern Church is the iconostasis, an elaborate screen or wall, entirely cutting off any view of the sanctuary or Altar. Directly behind the Holy Door of the iconostasis is the Altar, the 'throne'. The Eastern Christian is so filled with reverence and even fear of the Altar that he stands at a distance from it. No one below a deacon dare touch the Altar. And even the deacon dares to approach the Altar through the Holy Door only at certain specified times. This mystic veneration of the Altar is such a part of the Eastern spirituality[200].

The Sacred Congregation for Rites, in the Second Instruction on orderly carrying out the *Sacrosanctum Concilium*, reduced repetition of the gestures, and said about the genuflection of the celebrant:

> Celebrans genuflectit tantum :
> a) cum accedit ad Altare et ab eo recedit, si adest tabernaculum cum Sanctissimo Sacramento;
> b) post elevationem hostiae et post elevationem calicis;
> c) in fine Canonis, post doxologiam;
> d) ante Communionem, priusquam dicat Panem caelestem accipiam;
> e) expleta Communione fidelium, postquam hostias, quae forte superfuerint, in tabernaculo recondiderit. Reliquae genuflexiones omittuntur (No. 7)[201].

The above instruction was given in 1967 when the Tabernacle was still placed on the Altar. In the book, 'the Ceremonial of Bishops', numbers 68-69 we learn about the signs of reverence to the Altar during and outside the liturgy in the Church.

> A bow signifies reverence and honor toward persons or toward objects that represent persons. There are two kinds of bows, a bow of the head and a bow of the body:

---

[199] M. J. BEHEN, «The Christian Altar», 425.
[200] M. J. BEHEN, «The Christian Altar», 425.
[201] SACRA CONGREGATIO RITUUM, *Instructio altera: Tres abhinc annos*, ad exsecutionem constitutionis de sacra liturgia recte ordinandam, *AAS 59* (1967) 442-448, 444. tr. "The celebrant genuflects only: (a) On going to or leaving the Altar if there is a tabernacle containing the blessed sacrament; (b) after elevating the host and the chalice; (c) after the doxology at the end of the canon; (d) at communion, before the words *Panem caelestem accipiam*; (e) after the communion of the faithful, when he has placed the remaining hosts in the tabernacles. All other genuflections are omitted". Quoted from SC RITES (Consilium), «Instruction (second) *Tres abhinc annos*, on the orderly carrying out of the Constitution on the Liturgy, 4 May 1967», in *Documents on the Liturgy 1963 – 1979, Conciliar, Papal, and Curial Texts*, The Liturgical Press, Minnesota 1982, 135-140, 137.

(a) A bow of the head is made at the name of Jesus, the Blessed Virgin Mary, and the saint in whose honor the mass or the Liturgy of the hours is being celebrated.

(b) A bow of the body, or a deep bow, is made: to the Altar if there is no tabernacle with the blessed sacrament on the Altar; to the bishop, before and after incensation, as indicated in No. 91; whenever it is expressly called for by the rubrics of the various liturgical books (No. 68).

A genuflection, made by bending only the right knee to the ground, signifies adoration, and is therefore reserved for the blessed sacrament, whether exposed or reserved in the tabernacle, and for the holy cross from the time of the solemn adoration in the Liturgical celebration of the Easter Vigil (No. 69)[202].

The same document insists in number 72, "A deep bow is made to the Altar by all who enter the sanctuary, leave it, or pass before the Altar"[203]. In the General Instruction of the Roman Missal we see that the kissing of the Altar before and at the end of the mass always accompanied with a deep bow to the Altar[204].

Romano Guardini in his book 'Sacred Signs writes about the gestures of bowing, genuflection and kneeling. According to him,

> When a man feels proud of himself, he stands erect, draws himself to his full height, throws back his head and shoulders and says with every part of his body, I am bigger and more important than you. But when he is humble he feels his littleness, and lowers his head and shrinks into himself. He abases himself. And the greater the presence in which he stands the more deeply he abases himself; the smaller he becomes in his own eyes[205].

Bowing and genuflection help us to realize that God is so great and we are so small, so small that beside Him we seem hardly to exist. One has no need to be told that God's presence is not the place in which to stand on one's dignity. To appear less presumptuous, to be as little and low as we feel, we sink to our knees and thus sacrifice half our height; and to satisfy our hearts still further we bow down our heads, and our diminished stature speaks to God and says, 'Thou art the great God; I am nothing'[206].

---

[202] INTERNATIONAL COMMISSION ON ENGLISH IN THE LITURGY, *Ceremonial of Bishops: Revised by Decree of the Second Vatican Ecumenical Council and Published by Authority of Pope John Paul II*, 36.
[203] INTERNATIONAL COMMISSION ON ENGLISH IN THE LITURGY, *Ceremonial of Bishops: Revised by Decree of the Second Vatican Ecumenical Council and Published by Authority of Pope John Paul II*, 37.
[204] *Institutio Generalis Missalis Romani No. 49, 90, 123, 169, 173, 211, 251 & 256*, in *Missale Romanum Ex Decreto Sacrosancti Oecumenici Concilii Vaticani II, Instauratum auctoritate Pauli PP.VI promulgatum Ioannis Pauli PP. II cura recognitum*, 30, 39, 46, 51, 52, 56 & 61.
[205] R. GUARDINI, *Sacred Signs*, 14.
[206] R. GUARDINI, *Sacred Signs*, 14.

Guardini insists that let not the bending of our knees be a hurried gesture, an empty form:

> To kneel, in the soul's intention, is to bow down before God in deepest reverence. On entering a church, or in passing before the Altar, kneel down all the way without haste or hurry, putting your heart into what you do, and let your whole attitude say, 'Thou art the great God'. It is an act of humility, an act of truth, and every time you kneel it will do your soul good[207].

Therefore, bowing and genuflecting show that we are humbling ourselves before the presence of the almighty God in the Altar. These gestures are the signs of reverence and veneration towards the Altar which is Christ himself.

## 2.1.4. ADORNMENT OF THE ALTAR

The true, traditional, liturgical adornment of the Altar springs from the very nature of the Altar, that is, from its importance as the focal point of the whole Church, from its dignity and sanctity as the consecrated stone of sacrifice and the symbol of Christ himself. J. B. O'Connell says that the purpose of any adornment of the Altar should be to concentrate attention on, not distract attention from, the Altar itself, and what takes place on it:

> The purpose of adornment of the Altar should be, to enhance the beauty of the structure and emphasize its paramount place in the building. In the ornamentation of an Altar great care must be taken to respect the essential character of the Altar, and maintain its dignity, its austerity, its holiness. Its adornment must be worthy of the awesome character of an Altar, and nothing tawdry or pretty, artificial or sham should mar its sacredness[208].

The adornment should be restrained and dignified, something that teaches by its beauty and its symbolism. It must be such as not to spoil the architectural proportions, the essential lines and features of the Altar itself. J. B. O'Connell also says that an Altar loses its beauty precisely because of its expensive embellishment. According to him, when the liturgical laws of the adornment of an Altar are followed faithfully, then the maximum of majestic, dignified and austere beauty is attained[209].

Jungmann gives us a short history of the adornment of the Altar. The Altar was decked and decorated like a table; precious cloths were spread over it. In the Gothic

---

[207] R. GUARDINI, *Sacred Signs*, 15.
[208] J. B. O'CONNELL, *Church Building and Furnishing*, 182.
[209] J. B. O'CONNELL, *Church Building and Furnishing*, 182.

period, a decorative wall-painting was introduced over the Altar; the choice was crucifixion because it is the only representation or the principal one[210].

He further goes on to discuss the additions to the Altar in the history. The frontals (*antependia*) of our day which now cover usually the front of the Altar only, are the last vestiges of this sort of reverence. The next move was to add railings and steps. The most prominent of the marks of distinction given the Altar was the special shelter or canopy which surmounted it either by way of a *baldachin* or *testa* or by way of a fixed civory (*ciborium*). This covering over the Altar served to emphasize the special character of the table[211]. About the 11th century a few other rules were formed as the result of the introduction of a decorative structure ornamented with paintings, built either on the Altar table itself or immediately behind it, the so called retable[212]. The picture immediately behind or on the Altar itself was most often the picture one of the saint in whose honour the church was dedicated and whose relics, according to ancient principle, were buried there[213].

'Built of Living Stone', the document of the United States Bishops Conference says that since the Church teaches that 'the Altar is Christ', its composition should reflect the nobility, beauty, strength, and simplicity of the One it represents[214]. The same document quotes that *Sacrosanctum Concilium* called for the revision of legislation governing the material elements involved in the liturgy, particularly the construction of places of worship and Altars, the placement of the tabernacle and the baptistry, and the use of images and decoration[215]. In this topic of the adornment of the Altar, I limit myself with the Altar cloths, the Altar cross, the Altar candles and the Altar flowers. The other adornments like the Altar rails, steps, frontals (*antependia*), Civory (*Ciborium*), retables and reliquaries are not dealt with.

---

[210] J. JUNGMANN, *The Mass of the Roman Rite: Its Origin and Development Vol I*, 257.
[211] J. JUNGMANN, *The Mass of the Roman Rite: Its Origin and Development Vol I*, 257.
[212] J. JUNGMANN, *The Mass of the Roman Rite: Its Origin and Development Vol I*, 258.
[213] J. JUNGMANN, *The Mass of the Roman Rite: Its Origin and Development Vol I*, 258.
[214] UNITED STATES CONFERENCE OF CATHOLIC BISHOPS, *Built of Living Stones: Art, Architecture, and Worship*, in The Liturgy Documents Vol I, 433.
[215] UNITED STATES CONFERENCE OF CATHOLIC BISHOPS, *Built of Living Stones: Art, Architecture, and Worship*, in The Liturgy Documents Vol I, 431.

## 2.1.4.1. ALTAR CLOTHS

Clothing the Altar is clothing Christ himself. O'Connell says two ideas influenced the use of a cloth or cloths on the Altar; the symbolism of the clothing of Christ, represented by the Altar, and the symbolism of linen as a shroud for the Body of Christ[216]. Respect for the Sacred Species also demanded that they should be laid on fair linen. At first the Altar cloth was used only during the time of Mass, being spread by the deacons at the beginning of the service, and removed after it. It seems as though it has always been the custom for the Christian Altar to be clothed or vested during the celebration of the divine mysteries, at least from a very early date.

*LiberPontiticalis* says about Pope Silvester (314-335) who decreed that the sacrifice of the Altar is not to be celebrated on a silk or dyed cloth but only on a pure linen cloth just as the body of our Lord Jesus Christ was buried in a clean linen cloth.[217] Therefore, the Altar cloths symbolize the linens in which the body of Christ was wrapped, when it was laid in the sepulchre; or the purity and the devotion of the faithful: "For the fine linen are the justifications of saints" (Rev 19, 8). St. Optatus of Mileve (ca. 320-385) wrote in his work '*Schismate Donatistarum Adversus Parmenianum*', book vi, "*quis fidelium nescit in peragendis mysteriis ipsa linga linteamine cooperiri*"[218]. *Testamentum Domini Nostri Jesu Christi*, the Syrian text dating back to the 5th century, gives us a certain idea on an ideal Church. When describing the Altar linen it says, "*Velum ex bysso pura confectum habeat Altare, quoniam est immaculatum*"[219].

The doctrinal purpose of clothing the Altar is officially recognized in the Office of Ordination of Subdeacons.

> Altare quidem sanctae Ecclesiae ipse est Christus, teste Joanne qui in Apocalypsi sua Altare aureum se vidisse perhibet, stans ante thronum, in quo, et per quem oblationes fidelium Deo Patri consecrantur. Cujus Altaris pallae et corporalia sunt membra Christi, scilicet fideles Dei, quibus

---

[216] J. B. O'CONNELL, *Church Building and Furnishing*, 192.
[217] *Liber Pontificalis*, in *Worship in the Early Church: An Anthology of Historical Sources Vol 4*, ed. & tr. L. J. Johnson, Liturgical Press, Minnesota 2009, 53-58, 57.
[218] OPTAT DE MILÈVE, «Liber Sextus», 166. tr. "Every Christian knew that during the celebration of the mysteries the Altar is covered with a cloth". Quoted from OPTATUS, *The Work of St. Optatus: Against Donatists*, tr. O. R. V. Phillips, Longmans, Green & Co., London 1917, 251.
[219] *Testamentum Domini Nostri Jesu Christi*, ed. & tr. I. E. Rahmani, Sumptibus Francisci Kirchheim, Mouguintiae, 1899, 25. tr. "The Altar is to have a pure linen veil, one that is stainless". Quoted from *Testamentum Domini Nostri Jesu Christi*, in *Worship in the Early Church: An Anthology of Historical Sources Vol 3*, ed. & tr. L. J. Johnson, Liturgical Press, Minnesota 2009, 305-336, 308.

> Dominus, quasi vestimentis pretiosis circumdatur, ut ait Psalmista: Dominus regnavit, decorem indutus est[220].

Jungmann speaks about the usage and the practice of covering the Altar with cloths during the Eucharistic Celebration. He says that in the Roman Stational services in 7th century, after the Gospel, the pope again greets the throng with *Dominus vobiscum* and intones *Oremus*, but there is no prayer immediately following. Then the external preparations for the sacrifice of the Mass begin. First there is the covering of the Altar which until then has stood there, a stately but empty table, decorated only with a costly cloth that hung from the edges, the forerunner of the *antependium*. During the preparation for the offertory, a deacon takes the Altar cloth, lays it on the right side of the Altar and throws the open end to the second deacon at the other side in order to spread it over the entire top[221].

O'Connell says that the number of Altar cloths varied very much at different periods and in different places. At first there was only one linen cloth. Rome had adopted the use of three cloths by about the 8th or 9th century, but two were also in use there even as late as the 15th or 16th century[222]. Jungmann says that a number of Altar cloths were used already in the Carolingian period. The use of three linen Altar cloths besides the corporal became general only since the 17th century[223].

In the general blessings of *Rituale Romanum*, there is a blessing formula for Altar Linen. The prayer brings out the function and the Biblical background of the use of the Altar cloth.

> Benedictio Mapparum, sive Linteaminum Altaris: Domine, Deus omnipotens, qui Moysen famulum tuum, ornamenta ei linteamina fagere per quadraginta dies docuisti, quae etiam Maria textuit, et fecit in usum ministerii, et tabernaculi foederis: benedicere, sanctificare, et consecrare digneris haec

---

[220] *Pontificale Romanum Summorum Pontificum Jussu Editum a Benedicto XIV. et Leone XIII. pont. max. recognitum et castigatum*, Pustet, Regensburg 1891, 86. tr. "The cloths and corporals of the Altar are the members of Christ, God's faithful people, with whom the Lord is girded as with precious robes, as it were, with precious vestments as the psalmist says: 'The Lord is king, he is clothed with beauty'". Quoted from P. F. ANSON, *Churches their plan and Furnishing*, edd. T. F. Croft & H. A. Reinhold, The Bruce Publishing Company, Milwaukee 1948, 115.
[221] J. JUNGMANN, *The Mass of the Roman Rite: Its Origin and Development Vol I*, 71.
[222] J. B. O'CONNELL, *Church Building and Furnishing*, 192-193.
[223] J. JUNGMANN, *The Mass of the Roman Rite: Its Origin and Development Vol I*, 71.

> linteamina ad tegendum, involvendumque Altare gloriosissimi Filli tui Domini Jesu Christi....[224].

A manual of the ceremonies of a low mass says that the Altar linens must be blessed by the bishop or by one having the required faculties before they may be used[225]. The present General Instruction of the Roman Missal No. 117 says: *"Altare una saltem tobalea albi coloris cooperiatur"*[226], which insists that at least one white Altar cloth should be there on the Altar.

L. J. O'Connell says that the Altar linens should always be kept scrupulously clean as it is used on the Holy Altar[227]. Ignazio also quotes the blessing of the Altar cloths in his theological commentary on the dedication of a Church and an Altar. In the 1888 Roman Pontifical, the bishop, after having blessed the Altar cloths, ... goes to the sacristy where he takes off the cope[228].

Robinson when he is explaining the Christ Church Altar cloth, affirms that the Altar cloth attests to the saving power of Christ for all humanity[229]. Behen says that in the clothing of the Altar, we see the Lord Christ clothed with the precious vestments of His martyrs, confessors, and virgins, as the Church celebrates their feast days[230]. When the Altar is stripped on Holy Thursday, there is a profound sense of nakedness and abandonment[231].

Romano Guardini in his book 'Sacred Signs' writes about the Altar cloth. He tries to view it as a symbol of purity and respect.

> Good linen is a costly material. It is a sign of respect that we cover holy things with linen. When the Holy Sacrifice is offered, the uppermost covering of the Altar must be of fair linen. He says that the high Altar, in the Holy of Holies, represents the Altar in man's soul. The two Altars are inseparable and they are really, though mysteriously, the same Altar. The

---

[224] *Rituale Romanum: Pauli V. Pontificis Maximi Jussu Editum et a Benedicto XIV actum et castigatum*, Typis S. Congregationis de Propaganda Fide, Romae 1847, 244.
[225] *A Manual of the Ceremonies of Low Mass*, ed. L. Kuenzel, Frederick Pustet Co., New York 1930, 20.
[226] *Institutio Generalis Missalis Romani No. 117*, in *Missale Romanum Ex Decreto Sacrosancti Oecumenici Concilii Vaticani II, Instauratum auctoritate Pauli PP.VI promulgatum Ioannis Pauli PP. II cura recognitum*, 45.
[227] L. J. O'CONNELL, *The Book of ceremonies*, 19.
[228] M. C. IGNAZIO, *The Dedication of a Church and an Altar: A Theological Commentary*, 33.
[229] B. ROBINSON, «The Christ Church Cathedral Altar Cloth Controversy: Upanishadic Text and Eucharistic Context», in *Colloquium 39* (2007/1) 58-78, 64.
[230] M. J. BEHEN, «The Christian Altar», 427.
[231] J. P. BRADLEY, *The Catholic Layman's Library Vol 3*, 392.

authentic and perfect Altar in which Christ's sacrifice is offered is the union of them both[232].

Guardini tries to teach lessons for all the faithful from the Altar linen. Linen has much to teach us about the nature of purity. Purity is not the product of rude force or found in company with harsh manners. Its strength comes of its fineness and its orderliness is gentle. But at the same time, linen is also extremely strong. It was not always so clean and fine as it now is. In order to attain its present fragrant freshness it had to be washed and rewashed, and then bleached. Purity is not attained at the first. Purity is attained at the end of life, and achieved only by long and courageous effort. Therefore, the linen on the Altar, in its fine white, durability signifies to us both exquisite cleanness of heart and fibrous strength[233].

Thus the Altar cloth is the symbol of the members of Christ, the holy shroud of Christ's body, a reverential adornment for the sacred actions taking place on the Altar, and the symbol of the purity of the souls that are offering the sacrifice through the Holy Eucharist.

### 2.1.4.2. ALTAR CROSS

The Cross, with the figure of Christ, is the chief and the predominant element on the Altar. It is essential for the celebration of the Mass. It is placed on the Altar to call to the mind of the celebrant and the people, that the victim offered on the Altar is the same as was offered on the Cross. S. Maggiani says that the Symbol of the Cross in the Liturgy is very important and special as the liturgy is the expression of the paschal sacrifice. This is the sensible sign which makes the faithful see and realize the sacrifice of Christ which is represented by the Eucharistic sacrifice[234].

There are always five crosses inscribed as marks on the Altar stone. O'Connell says that to mark the place where the stone is signed with blessed water and anointed at its consecration it is usual to incise five crosses on the table one at each corner and one in the middle. These crosses made their appearance very early, as early in the 6th or 7th

---

[232] R. GUARDINI, *Sacred Signs*, 34.
[233] R. GUARDINI, *Sacred Signs*, 34-35.
[234] S. MAGGIANI, «Il symbolo della Croce nello Spazio Liturgico», in *Rivista Liturgica 101* (2014/1) 115-117.

century. These five crosses are normally the permanent marks of the consecration of the Altar[235]. According to Jungmann, in the 11$^{th}$ century the crucifix was brought to the Altar, a prescription of law still maintained to this day[236].

O'Connell gives a short history of the appearance of the Cross on the Altar. The first clear mention of a Cross at the head of a procession in Rome is at the coronation of Charlemagne (800), who presented such a Cross to Pope Leo III (795-816). After that time the use of a Cross at the head of a procession became quite common and a Cross was also carried before the Pope. This latter practice spread to archbishops, and was fairly general about the 11$^{th}$ century. Before the 11$^{th}$ century the Cross, for Mass, was not placed on the Altar. The processional Cross was often used and was fixed, during Mass, behind the Altar or at its side, or held there by a server. In the 11$^{th}$ century the Cross, as we now know it, began to make its appearance on the table of the Altar[237].

Ceremonial of Bishops number 129 says that it is preferable that the processional Cross be placed near the Altar and serve as the Altar Cross[238]. G. S. Duncan says that the Altar as an expression of the Cross is often iterated by a decorative bas-relief or engraving on the frontal[239]. The General Instruction of the Roman Missal refers several times the Crucifix on the Altar[240]. Especially number 308 says that it is appropriate to keep an Altar cross, which calls to mind for the faithful the saving Passion of the Lord. It also adds that the cross should remain near the Altar even outside of liturgical celebrations.

> Item super Altare vel prope ipsum crux, cum effigie Christi crucifixi, habeatur, quæ a populo congregato bene conspiciatur. Expedit ut huiusmodi crux, ad salutiferam Domini passionem in mentem fidelium revocandam, etiam extra celebrationes liturgicas prope Altare permaneat[241].

---

[235] J. B. O'CONNELL, *Church Building and Furnishing*, 137.
[236] J. JUNGMANN, *The Mass of the Roman Rite: Its Origin and Development Vol I*, 259.
[237] J. B. O'CONNELL, *Church Building and Furnishing*, 201-204.
[238] INTERNATIONAL COMMISSION ON ENGLISH IN THE LITURGY, *Ceremonial of Bishops: Revised by Decree of the Second Vatican Ecumenical Council and Published by Authority of Pope John Paul II*, 52.
[239] G. S. DUNCAN, *The Church Building as a Sacred Place: Beauty, Transcendence, and the Eternal*, 21.
[240] *Institutio Generalis Missalis Romani No. 117, 122, 188 & 350*, in *Missale Romanum Ex Decreto Sacrosancti Oecumenici Concilii Vaticani II, Instauratum auctoritate Pauli PP.VI promulgatum Ioannis Pauli PP. II cura recognitum*, 45, 46, 53 & 76.
[241] *Institutio Generalis Missalis Romani No. 308*, in *Missale Romanum Ex Decreto Sacrosancti Oecumenici Concilii Vaticani II, Instauratum auctoritate Pauli PP.VI promulgatum Ioannis Pauli PP. II cura recognitum*, 70.

In 'Built of Living Stones' regarding church furnishings, one can see the purpose of keeping the Cross on the Altar.

> The Cross with the image of Christ crucified is a reminder of Christ's paschal mystery. It draws us into the mystery of suffering and makes tangible our belief that our suffering when united with the passion and death of Christ leads to redemption. There should be a Crucifix 'positioned either on the Altar or near it, and ... clearly visible to the people gathered there.'[242].

Valenziano says that in the Eucharistic Liturgy, like the *Evangelarium* signifies the presence of Christ because His Word is in it, so also the Cross signifies the presence of Christ because the sacrifice that is offered on the Altar is the same sacrifice of the Cross[243].

The Sacred Congregation in explaining the question, '*Estne adhuc ponenda crux in Altare versus Populum?*', says that there are three possibilities: to place the processional Cross before the Altar, with the face turned toward the celebrant, to have a large, pendant Cross or to have a large Cross affixed to the apse wall. In addition, the explanation adds that in the last two instances another Cross for the Altar is not required, the single large Cross is enough. The Cross is also incensed as well when the Altar is incensed.

> Extra Altare triplex datur possibilitas: ponendi Crucem processionalem ante Altare, facie versa ad celebrantem, quod non simper cum aliis elementis presbyterii bene cohaeret; adhibendi magnam Crucem ex alto pendentem vel in pariete absidis positam. Neque, in ultimis duo bus casibus necessaria est altera Crux pro Altari, sed sufficit unica magna Crux, quae, in celebrationibus versus populum, non incensatur primo loco, sed cum sacerdos, Altare circumiens, coram ipsa sistat ad alteram Altaris faciem[244].

By insisting and giving possibilities to keep the Cross near that Altar, we come to know the real importance of the Altar Cross. The General Instruction of the Roman Missal insists that great attention should be given to Altar cross as it is directly associated with the Altar and the Eucharistic celebration.

---

[242] United States Conference of Catholic Bishops, *Built of Living Stones (2000)*, 441.
[243] C. Valenziano, *L'anello della sposa: Mistagogia Eucaristica I. Modulazione circolare del Rito*, Centro Liturgico Vincenziano, Roma 2005, 73.
[244] Sacra Congregatio Rituum, «Ad Instructionem 101», *Notitiae 2* (1966) 21-22.

> Insuper omni cura attendendum est ad ea quæ directe cum Altari et celebratione eucharistica conectuntur, uti sunt, ex. gr., Crux Altaris et Crux quæ in processione defertur[245].

J. Ratzinger in his book 'the Spirit of Liturgy', while explaining the Altar and direction of liturgical prayer, speaks about the Altar Cross.

> Facing East, as we heard, was linked with the 'sign of the Son of Man', with the Cross, which announces the Lord's second Coming. That is why very early on the East was linked with the sign of the Cross. Where a direct common turning toward the east is not possible, the Cross came to serve as the interior 'East' of faith. It should stand in the middle of the Altar and be the common point of focus for both priest and praying community[246].

The Crucifix at the centre of the Altar recalls so many splendid meanings of the Sacred Liturgy, which can be summarized by referring to the Catechism of the Catholic Church number 618:

> The Cross is the unique sacrifice of Christ, the 'one mediator between God and men'. But because in his incarnate divine person he has in some way united himself to every man, 'the possibility of being made partners, in a way known to God, in the paschal mystery' is offered to all men. He calls his disciples to 'take up (their) Cross and follow (him)', for 'Christ also suffered for (us), leaving (us) an example so that (we) should follow in his steps.' In fact Jesus desires to associate with his redeeming sacrifice those who were to be its first beneficiaries. This is achieved supremely in the case of his mother, who was associated more intimately than any other person in the mystery of his redemptive suffering. Apart from the Cross there is no other ladder by which we may get to heaven[247].

Crucifix is the principle ornament of the Altar. The Cross must be placed that it can be clearly visible to all at the Mass. Thus we see the importance of the Altar Cross. It is the sacrifice of the Cross that is celebrated and perpetuated in the Altar sacrifice. Therefore, when the faithful see and venerate the cross, they bring to their mind the original significance of the Altar and associate the actions on the Altar with the cross.

---

[245] *Institutio Generalis Missalis Romani No. 350,* in *Missale Romanum Ex Decreto Sacrosancti Oecumenici Concilii Vaticani II, Instauratum auctoritate Pauli PP.VI promulgatum Ioannis Pauli PP. II cura recognitum,* 76.
[246] J. RATZINGER, *The Spirit of Liturgy,* tr. J. Saward, Ignatius Press, San Francisco 2000, 83.
[247] *Catechism of the Catholic Church,* Mambo Press, Gweru 1992, n.618.

## 2.1.4.3. ALTAR CANDLES

In Catholic Churches throughout the world, we see the Altar candles as one of the adornments of the Altar. We can try to see the significance and symbolism behind the Altar candles. There would seem to be no documentary evidence that lighted candles were placed on the Altar before the 10th century or even later[248].

As long as the struggle with paganism continued, candles were permitted in Christian worship only for practical reasons. In the face of initial opposition, it became a popular Christian practice in the 4th Century to light lamps and candles at the graves of Christian martyrs. Extended to images and places of pilgrimage the practice has survived to this day especially in Latin Countries as 'Votive Candles'[249]. Pecklers also mentions in his book 'Worship', the pilgrims using the votive candles when they missed the Sunday mass[250].

Jungmann in his book, 'The Mass of the Roman Rite', writes about the usage of lighted candles. As a sign of honour, fire in the form of torches and braziers were carried in front of the Roman emperor and high officials. After the 4th Century, this honour was transferred to the Pope, the Roman clergy and the bishops. Then there emerged the practice of the lighted candles carried before the celebrant, and these were set down near the Altar[251]. However, according to O'Connell;

> At first all candlesticks for ceremonial use were carried and during Mass were set down, temporarily, not on the Altar, but beside it or behind it or were held by servers. Only after a thousand years or more when the inviolability of the Altar was fading from memory, the civory was falling into desuetude, and relic shrines and retables were invading the table of the Altar, did the cross and candlesticks find their way on to it; and then, at first, only temporarily, during a function[252].

The number of candles used around the Altar at Mass varied greatly from century to century and from place to place, and for different days. For certain votive Masses, for symbolical reasons (e.g., seven candles for a Mass of the Holy Spirit) three,

---

[248] P. F. ANSON, *Churches their plan and Furnishing*, 106.
[249] G. PODHRADSKY, *New Dictionary of the Liturgy*, ed. L. Sheppard, Geoffrey Chapman, London 1967, 47.
[250] K. F. PECKLERS, *Worship: A New Century Theology*, Continuum, London 2003, 146.
[251] J. JUNGMANN, *The Mass of the Roman Rite: Its Origin and Development Vol I*, 68-69.
[252] J. B. O'CONNELL, *Church Building and Furnishing*, 204-205.

five, seven, twelve and even twenty-four candles were sometimes lit[253]. At the Pope's stational Mass, there were two or four candles on the Altar. Jungmann says, "….two to four candles are found sufficient, and they stand on the Altar"[254].

According to O'Connell, by the middle of the 13th century seven candles had made their appearance, on the table of the Altar, at a solemn papal Mass, at least on great days. It became exaggerated in the 17th century. Candlesticks were often made, in large Churches, of precious metals and were of marvellous workmanship. In design and ornamentation, the Altar candlesticks should be in keeping with those of the Church and the Altar. Their size will depend on the proportions of the Altar and cross. They should not overshadow the Cross, and those nearest the Cross must not exceed the base of the Cross in height[255].

The position of the candle on the Altar is given in the Ceremonial of Bishops number 129, "The candlesticks are placed near the Altar or on a side table or at some nearby place in the Sanctuary"[256]. The General Instruction of the Roman Missal in No. 117 & 307 describes their location:

> Candelabra, quæ pro singulis actionibus liturgicis, venerationis et festivæ celebrationis causa, requiruntur (No. 117), aut super Altare, aut circa ipsum, attenta structura tum Altaris tum presbyterii, opportune collocentur, ita ut totum concinne componatur, neque fideles impediantur ab iis facile conspiciendis, quæ super Altare aguntur vel deponuntur[257].

The Congregation of the Sacred Rites in executing the *Sacrosanctum Concilium*, in the first instruction number 94 speaks about the placement of the candles. *"Crux et candelabra quae pro singulis actionibus liturgicis in Altari requiruntur, de iudicio Ordinarii loci, etiam iuxta ipsum poni possunt"*[258].

---

[253] J. JUNGMANN, *The Mass of the Roman Rite: Its Origin and Development Vol I*, 130.
[254] J. JUNGMANN, *The Mass of the Roman Rite: Its Origin and Development Vol I*, 203.
[255] J. B. O'CONNELL, *Church Building and Furnishing*, 205.
[256] INTERNATIONAL COMMISSION ON ENGLISH IN THE LITURGY, *Ceremonial of Bishops: Revised by Decree of the Second Vatican Ecumenical Council and Published by Authority of Pope John Paul II*, 52.
[257] *Institutio Generalis Missalis Romani No. 307*, in *Missale Romanum Ex Decreto Sacrosancti Oecumenici Concilii Vaticani II, Instauratum auctoritate Pauli PP.VI promulgatum Ioannis Pauli PP. II cura recognitum*, 69-70. "The candles, which are required at every liturgical service out of reverence and on account of the festiveness of the celebration (No. 117), are to be appropriately placed either on or around the Altar in a way suited to the design of the Altar and the sanctuary so that the whole may be well balanced and not interfere with the faithful's clear view of what takes place at the Altar or what is placed on it". Quoted from *General Instruction of the Roman Missal: Liturgy Documentary Series 2*, 103.
[258] SACRA CONGREGATIO RITUUM, *Instructio 94: ad exsecutionem constitutionis de sacra liturgia recte ordinandam*, 898. tr. "At the discretion of the Ordinary, the cross and the candlesticks required on the

In discussing the material of the Candle, O'Connell says that candles used for cultural purposes must be real wax, because of traditional usage and because of the symbolism attached to wax. Oil lamps may not be substituted for them. If pure beeswax candles are difficult to obtain, those with some mixture of vegetable fats may be used[259].

The United States Conference of Catholic Bishops, in the document *Built of Living Stones number* 93, speaks about the material of the Candle and forbids the use of electrical lights:

> Candles for liturgical use should be made of a material that provides 'a living flame without being smoky or noxious'. To safeguard authenticity and the full symbolism of light, 'electric lights as a substitute for candles are not permitted'[260].

For some centuries only beeswax was the material of the candles used in the Church. Ennodius, in his description on '*Benedictio Cerei*' gives the symbolism of using beeswax candles. He says that the pure wax extracted by bees from flowers symbolizes the pure flesh of Christ received from His Virgin Mother, the wick signifies the soul of Christ, and the flame represents His divinity[261]. The Catechism of the Catholic Church number 1189 discusses about the symbolism of the materials used in the Liturgy;

> The liturgical celebration involves signs and symbols relating to creation (candles, water, fire), human life (washing, anointing, breaking bread) and the history of salvation (the rites of the Passover). Integrated into the world of faith and taken up by the power of the Holy Spirit, these cosmic elements, human rituals, and gestures of remembrance of God become bearers of the saving and sanctifying action of Christ[262].

As a sacramental the candle, which is considered as a Symbol of Christ, has several meanings. Podhradsky says that in storms blessed candles are lit and the blessing of St. Blaise is given with two crossed candles[263].

---

Altar for the various liturgical rites may also be placed next to it". Quoted from SC Rites (Consilium), «Instruction (first) *Inter Oecumenici,* on the orderly carrying out of the Constitution on the Liturgy, 26 September 1964», 109.

[259] J. B. O'Connell, *Church Building and Furnishing*, 204-213.
[260] United States Conference of Catholic Bishops, *Built of Living Stones (2000)*, 442.
[261] Magni Felicis Ennodii, «Benedictio Cerei», in *Opera Omnia*, ed. G. Hartel, (Corpus Scriptorum Ecclesiasticorum 6), Vindobonae 1882, 415-422.
[262] *Catechism of the Catholic Church 1189.*
[263] G. Podhradsky, *New Dictionary of the Liturgy*, 47.

M. C. Ignazio says that the Church resplendent in light is a symbol of the Church, illumined by Christ, and of the heavenly Jerusalem whose lamp is the Lamb[264]. In dedication rite, it would be wrong, however, to believe that the 'rite of light' has only a decorative function at the banquet table. It has a deep theological meaning: Christ is the 'light of the world' (Jn 8, 12), 'a revealing light to the Gentiles' (Lk 2, 32), the only true light of the Church. That light prefigures the last condition of the human race, proper to the heavenly Jerusalem (Rev 21, 10; 22-23)[265].

In *Ordo Dedicationis Ecclesiae et Altaris* we see, the bishop pronounces a formula which recalls the Easter Vigil's diaconal admonition concerning the lighting of candles. Taken as a whole, however, the formula is a virtual synthesis of Chapter 1 of the Constitution on the Church[266]. "*Lumen Christi in Ecclesia refulgeat, ut omnes gentes plentitudinem veritatis attingant*"[267].

In the document *Built of Living Stones*, number 92 explains the use of candles in the Liturgy and the symbolic meaning behind it. It says that candle is a symbol of the risen Christ and reminder of Baptism:

> Candles, which are signs of reverence and festivity, are to be used at every liturgical service. The living flame of the candle, symbolic of the risen Christ, reminds people that in baptism they are brought out of darkness into God's marvellous light.... Candles placed in floor-standing bases or on the Altar should be arranged so they do not obscure the view of the ritual action in the sanctuary, especially the action at the Altar[268].

Romano Guardini in his work 'Sacred Signs', writes about the meaning of using the Candles in the Liturgy:

> The Candle light seems a symbol of selfless generosity. It stands so unwavering in its place, so erect, so clear and disinterested, in perfect readiness to be of service. It stands, where it is well to stand, before God. It stands in its appointed place, self-consumed in light and warmth. Yes, of course the candle is unconscious of what it does. It has no soul. But we can

---

[264] M. C. IGNAZIO, *The Dedication of a Church and an Altar: A Theological Commentary*, 31.
[265] M. C. IGNAZIO, *The Dedication of a Church and an Altar: A Theological Commentary*, 30.
[266] M. C. IGNAZIO, *The Dedication of a Church and an Altar: A Theological Commentary*, 31.
[267] *Ordo Dedicationis Ecclesiae et Altaris, Pontificale Romanum, Ex Decreto Sacrosancti Ecumenici Concili Vaticani II Instauratum Auctoritate Pauli PP. VI Promulgatum*, 51. tr. "Light of Christ, shine forth in the Church and bring all nations to the fullness of truth". Quoted from *Dedication of a Church and an Altar*, 57.
[268] UNITED STATES CONFERENCE OF CATHOLIC BISHOPS, *Built of Living Stones (2000)*, 441-442.

give it a soul by making it an expression of our own attitude. Stir up in yourself the same generous readiness to be used[269].

He explains the symbolism of Candles very practical and applicable for the lives of the faithful. He is giving a very clear idea saying:

> Let the clean, spare, serviceable candle bespeak your own attitude. Let your readiness grow into steadfast loyalty. Even as this candle, O Lord, would I stand in your presence. Do not weaken in or try to evade your vocation. Persevere. Do not keep asking why and to what purpose. To be consumed in truth and love, in light and warmth, for God, is the profoundest purpose of human life[270].

Thus the Altar candles are the symbol of light of Christ, the selfless generosity of God in showing His love for the humanity and reminder for all the participants to bear the light of Christ. The vision of Guardini about the Altar candles is also enlightening.

## 2.1.4.4. ALTAR FLOWERS

A long history of flowers as adornment for the Altar, before statues, at shrines, and pilgrimage centres exists in the Catholic Church. Thus they are associated with a sense of joy and festivity[271]. The use of flowers for the temporary decoration of an Altar is widespread in the Western Church. O'Connell says that in the early centuries flowers were used to adorn the tombs of the martyrs and, later, the *confessio*, where the body of a saint was enshrined. From the 4th century, there are references to the use of flowers in the church and around Altars. Garlands were hung on the walls, on columns, on doors, and adorned the civory and the ambos. Flowers and sweet-smelling herbs were scattered on the church floor[272].

R. Kieckhefer in his book, 'Theology in Stone' writes about the floral decoration in the churches. He says that from the era of Constantine we have the mosaic from the floor of the large double church excavated at Aquileia; here is the representation of an offertory procession in which men and women are bringing not

---

[269] R. GUARDINI, *Sacred Signs*, 23.
[270] R. GUARDINI, *Sacred Signs*, 23.
[271] J. P. LANG, *Dictionary of the Liturgy*, Catholic Book Publishing Corp., New York 1989, 212.
[272] J. B. O'CONNELL, *Church Building and Furnishing*, 196-197.

only bread and wine, but also grapes, flowers, and a bird[273]. J. P. Lang says that the floral decorations are symbolically interpreted throughout the centuries. For instance, some of the figurative meanings are: 'the tulip, prayer; the myrtle, the state of virginity; the hawthorne, hope; the violet, humility; the hyacinth, peace and power'[274]. In the same way G. D. Huck also gives various symbolic meanings giving by the Christians. Garland of flowers signifies the paradisial state of the saints and various flowers used to designate persons and virtues[275].

P. F. Anson says that the floral decorations seem to have been used in Christian Churches from an early period, but they were confined to garlands hung from the walls and columns, or strewn upon the floor. During the Middle Ages it was a common custom to strew sweet-smelling herbs, such as rosemary or bay leaves, on the pavement[276].

The United States Conference of Catholic Bishops, in the document *Built of Living Stones number* 129 speaks about the flower plants in the church surroundings to create the atmosphere of beauty and serenity.

> The use of living flowers and plants, rather than artificial greens, serves as a reminder of the gift of life God has given to the human community. Planning for plants and flowers should include not only the procurement and placement but also the continuing care needed to sustain living things[277].

*Memoriale Rituum* of Benedict XIII says about use of flowers and candles to decorate the high Altar on the Holy Thursday. "*Locus ipse ab Altari majori distinctus, et decenter velis pretiosis, non tamen nigris, et luminibus ac floribus ornatus, sine Reliquiis aut imaginibus Sanctorum*"[278]. In describing the stripping of the Altar after the Holy Thursday celebration, the same document says: "*Clerici recipient tabeleas, et amovent ab Altari vasa florum, pallium, tapete etc., adeo ut in Altari non remaneant nisi*

---

[273] R. KIECKHEFER, *Theology in Stone: Church Architecture from Byzantium to Berkeley*, Oxford University Press, New York 2004, 29.
[274] J. P. LANG, *Dictionary of the Liturgy*, 213.
[275] G. D. HUCK, «Symbolism of Flowers», in *The New Catholic Encyclopedia of Religion Vol 5*, ed. W. J. McDonald, McGraw-Hill Book Company, New York 1967, 981-982, 982.
[276] P. F. ANSON, *Churches their plan and Furnishing*, 125.
[277] UNITED STATES CONFERENCE OF CATHOLIC BISHOPS, *Built of Living Stones (2000)*, 448.
[278] *Memoriale Rituum: pro aliquibus praestantioribus sacris functionibus persolvendis in minoribus ecclesiis Benedicti XIII Pont. Max. jussu editum Benedicti Papae XV auctoritatae recognitum*, Typis Polyglottis Vaticanis, Romae 1950, 41.

*Crux et candelabra cum candelis exstinctis*"[279]. This description shows the use of flower vases during the Holy Thursday service that are kept on the Altar. The Ceremonial of the Roman Rite (1962), says that the flowers on the Altar is not necessary. They are not used in the large churches of Rome. However, there is no law against them at certain times. It says that they should be used with the greatest restraint[280].

The General Instruction of the Roman Missal number 305 gives us a clear instruction for the floral decorations in the sanctuary.

> In Altaris ornatu moderatio servetur. Tempore Adventus Altare floribus ornetur ea moderatione, quæ indoli huius temporis conveniat, quin tamen plenam lætitiam Nativitatis Domini præveniat. Tempore Quadragesimæ Altare floribus ornari prohibetur. Excipiuntur tamen dominica Lætare (IV in Quadragesima), sollemnitates et festa. Florum ornatus semper sit temperatus, et potius quam supra mensam Altaris, circa illud disponatur[281].

L. J. O'Connell, former master of Ceremonies, in his book of Ceremonies says that the flowers may be used on the Altar for ornamentation, but they should not detract from the Altar itself or its essentials and he adds that the artificial flowers are to be discouraged[282]. P. F. Anson insists that flowers are only ornaments and subsidiary. He condemns making the Altar as a mere place of decoration and a flower stand:

> Flowers should be used in church and especially on the Altar with the greatest restraint. They are an ornament and, though they may be and are very beautiful, they are entirely subsidiary and their use is intended to mark a special degree of festivity. It is very unbecoming to make the Altar which, as the hallowed stone of sacrifice and the dwelling place of God under the Sacramental Species, should be a place of awe and dignity a mere stand for flowers[283].

---

[279] *Memoriale Rituum: pro aliquibus praestantioribus sacris functionibus persolvendis in minoribus ecclesiis Benedicti XIII Pont. Max. jussu editum Benedicti Papae XV auctoritatae recognitum*, 48.

[280] A. FORTESCUE & J. B. O'CONNELL, *The Ceremonies of the Roman Rite Described*, Burns & Oates Ltd., London 1962, 29.

[281] *Institutio Generalis Missalis Romani No. 305*, in *Missale Romanum Ex Decreto Sacrosancti Oecumenici Concilii Vaticani II, Instauratum auctoritate Pauli PP.VI promulgatum Ioannis Pauli PP. II cura recognitum*, 69. tr. "Moderation should be observed in the decoration of the Altar. During Advent the floral decoration of the Altar should be marked by a moderation suited to the character of this season, without expressing prematurely the full joy of the Nativity of the Lord. During Lent it is forbidden for the Altar to be decorated with flowers. Laetare Sunday (Fourth Sunday of Lent), solemnities, and feasts are exceptions. Floral decorations should always be done with moderation and placed around the Altar rather than on its mensa". Quoted from *General Instruction of the Roman Missal: Liturgy Documentary Series 2*, 102.

[282] L. J. O'CONNELL, *The Book of ceremonies*, 16.

[283] P. F. ANSON, *Churches their plan and Furnishing*, 125.

But at the same time, Anson clarifies that flowers are offerings, not mere decorations. Their position should indicate this. They should stand before or round the Altar not on it[284]. Jungmann says "Like the flowers and candles, like the beauty of the vestments and the sound of the organ, the clouds of incense rising to the ceiling and filling the whole Church with their sweet smell are intended to aid the senses in grasping the greatness of the feast"[285]. O'Connell gives certain directions for the arrangement of flowers in the church. The following are some points which he suggests as practical hints:

> (1) The quality of the flowers is much more important than their quantity; a few vases of well- arranged, suitable flowers is the ideal. Only large flowers are suitable for a high Altar, they have dignity and can be seen even at a distance, and they should be flowers that last well when cut and do not exhale a heavy perfume.
> (2) It is becoming when the colour of the flowers is in harmony with the liturgical furnishings (the colour of the Office); sometimes a complementary colour looks well. Flowers of one colour only are usually best, to avoid a blurred effect at a distance.
> (3) The artistic arrangement of flowers is a special art; use long stemmed, fresh flowers, very loosely arranged, with plenty of suitable foliage; avoid overcrowding the vase[286].

R. Kieckhefer, quoting from the German writer Horst Wenzel, says about the experience of a medieval Christian in a church, which is a place for manifestation of God to each of the senses:

> To the eyes, in its dazzling artwork and in the ritual acts performed;
> To the ears, through both word and music;
> To the nose, in "divine fragrance" of incense and flowers;
> To the taste, in the Eucharist, said to give a foretaste of God's sweetness;
> To the touch, in the kiss of peace and the kissing of various sacred objects, and especially in extra liturgical contact with relics. If everyday life is perhaps gray and filled with workaday cacophony, the church is meant as a place where one can experience the beautiful as an emanation of divine beauty[287].

As he says the flowers are sensible signs to the eyes and nose. P. F. Anson discusses forbidding the use of artificial flowers of cheap materials. The *Caeremoniale Episcoporum* implies that the material should be silk, and cheap paper or calico flowers

---

[284] P. F. ANSON, *Churches their plan and Furnishing*, 125.
[285] J. JUNGMANN, *The Mass of the Roman Rite: Its Origin and Development Vol I*, 317.
[286] J. B. O'CONNELL, *Church Building and Furnishing*, 199.
[287] R. KIECKHEFER, *Theology in Stone: Church Architecture from Byzantium to Berkeley*, 98.

should be avoided. The best artificial flowers are of metal or gilded wood. They look very effective, and last longer than those made of silk[288]. J. P. Lang says that artificial flowers are certainly out of place, because cut and natural flowers resemble a form of sacrifice, since they wither and must be replaced[289].

N. Stenta states that the liturgy is life and loves life; it therefore desires living flowers and plants in church. He gives the reason for the Altar flowers to be present near the Altar. As the sanctuary lamp continuously burns before the tabernacle, so do flowers bloom, as a fragrant prayer, before the abode of the Redeemer. The flowers in Church have a threefold role: They are a highly expressive symbol of virtue, of man's transient life, of eternal bliss, etc. They are the representatives of irrational nature at the Sacrifice of the Redemption. They are a significant offering, a vicarious dying-with-Christ of mankind[290].

O'Connell insists that flowers in Church should speak to us by their fresh beauty and their symbolism of their Maker, of his craftsmanship and goodness, and of his other perfections. They should enhance the beauty of the Altar and its setting, not distract attention from it or disfigure it[291]. Thus, the Altar flowers are adding beauty to the Altar, though they are not essential, they are used with symbolic meaning and with aesthetics. They are the symbols of the selfless sacrifice of Christ, the fragrance of the prayer of the soul, a total offering to God and thus all flowers should be natural and modest.

## 2.2. SYMBOLISM OF THE ALTAR

The United States Conference of Catholic Bishops, in the document *Built of Living Stones number 26* brings out the importance of the signs and symbols used in the Liturgy.

> Just as Christ invited those who heard him to share his personal union with the Father through material signs, so Christ leads the Church through these same signs in the liturgy from visible to the invisible. As a result, effective liturgical signs have a teaching function and encourage full, conscious, and

---

[288] P. F. ANSON, *Churches their plan and Furnishing*, 126.
[289] J. P. LANG, *Dictionary of the Liturgy*, 212.
[290] N. STENTA, «Use of flowers in the Liturgy», in *Orate Fratres 4* (1930/11) 462-469, 463-464.
[291] J. B. O'CONNELL, *Church Building and Furnishing*, 196-200.

active participation, express and strengthen faith, and lead people to God....
the liturgy and its signs and symbols do not exercise merely a teaching
function. They also touch and move a person to conversion of heart and not
simply to enlightenment of mind[292].

Many symbolisms can be derived from the Altar. Edsman says that the Altar could be seen as a symbol of the heavenly throne or of Christ himself, his cross or his grave[293]. G. S. Duncan says that the Altar can also symbolize the table of the Last supper, the Altar of the Temple of Jerusalem, the Cross of Calvary, the tomb of Christ's burial and Resurrection, and the Altar in heaven[294].

Some authors give some allegorical meaning to the Altar. Jungmann speaks about Pseudo-Dionysius, one of the first to champion the liturgical allegorization at the start of the 6th century. His Neo-Platonic thinking inspired not only the method but, to a degree, also the content of his interpretation of the liturgy. However, he uses the allegorical system to explain only isolated moments in the Mass, as when he interprets the priest's coming from the Altar to distribute Communion as an image of the Incarnation[295].

Theodore of Mopsuestia (d. 428) and the Syrian Narsai (d. 502), who understand, for instance, that the carrying of the gift-offerings to the Altar as the burial of Jesus, the transubstantiation as His Resurrection, and the breaking of the consecrated bread as the appearance of the Risen Saviour[296]. Behen states that at the heart of the Christian life stands the Altar. For each Christian, the Altar means life, redemption, and resurrection. The Altar is our passage from death to life. There is no grace given to man but flows from the inexhaustible riches of the Altar[297].

## 2.2.1. THE SYMBOL OF COVENANT AND COMMUNION

The communion of man with God is the object of our Christian Vocation. *Gaudium et Spes 18* says, *"Deus enim hominem vocavit et vocat ut Ei in perpetua*

---

[292] UNITED STATES CONFERENCE OF CATHOLIC BISHOPS, *Built of Living Stones: Art, Architecture, and Worship*, 24.
[293] C. EDSMAN, «Altar», in *The Encyclopedia of Religion Vol I*, 225.
[294] G. S. DUNCAN, *The Church Building as a Sacred Place: Beauty, Transcendence, and the Eternal*, 20.
[295] J. JUNGMANN, *The Mass of the Roman Rite: Its Origin and Development Vol I*, 87.
[296] J. JUNGMANN, *The Mass of the Roman Rite: Its Origin and Development Vol I*, 87.
[297] M. J. BEHEN, «The Christian Altar», 422.

*incorruptibilis vitae divinae communione tota sua natura adhaereat*"[298]. The same document says in number 19, "*Dignitatis humanae eximia ratio in vocatione hominis ad communionem cum Deo consistit*"[299].

The Vatican Council in the Decree on the Mission activity of the Church *Ad Gentes 3* says that Communion with God leads to communion with the neighbour and for realizing that communion He sent His only Son.

> Deus autem ad pacem seu communionem Secum stabiliendam fraternamque societatem inter homines, eosque peccatores, componendam, in historiam hominum novo et definitivo modo intrare decrevit mittendo Filium suum in carne nostra, ut homines per Illum eriperet de potestate tenebrarum ac Satanae et in Eo mundum Sibi reconciliaret[300].

The Decree on the Ecumenism, *Unitatis Redintegratio 7*, formulates the doctrine of the communion in the Trinitarian mode reminding all that the faithful should be in communion with the Trinity and with their neighbours;

> Meminerint omnes christifideles se Christianorum unionem eo melius promovere, immo exercere, quo puriorem secundum Evangelium vitam degere studeant. Quo enim arctiore communione cum Patre, Verbo et Spiritu unientur, eo intimius atque facilius mutuam fraternitatem augere valebunt[301].

---

[298] CONCILIUM OECUMENICUM VATICANUM II, Constitutio Pastoralis de Ecclesia in mundo huius temporis *Guadium et Spes 18*, *AAS 58* (1966) 1025-1118, 1038. tr. "For God has called man and still calls him so that with his entire being he might be joined to Him in an endless sharing of a divine life beyond all corruption". Quoted from VATICAN COUNCIL II, *Guadium et Spes*: in *The Conciliar and Post Conciliar Documents* 1, 918.

[299] CONCILIUM OECUMENICUM VATICANUM II, Constitutio Pastoralis de Ecclesia in mundo huius temporis *Guadium et Spes 19*, 1038 tr. "The root reason for human dignity lies in man's call to communion with God". Quoted from VATICAN COUNCIL II, *Guadium et Spes*, 918.

[300] CONCILIUM OECUMENICUM VATICANUM II, Decretum de Activitate Missionali Ecclesiae *Ad Gentes 3*, *AAS* 58 (1966) 947-990, 949. tr. "Now God, in order to establish peace or the communion of sinful human beings with Himself, as well as to fashion them into a fraternal community, did ordain to intervene in human history in a way both new and finally sending His Son, clothed in our flesh, in order that through Him He might snatch men from the power of darkness and Satan and reconcile the world to Himself in Him". Quoted from VATICAN COUNCIL II, *Ad Gentes*: in *The Conciliar and Post Conciliar Documents* 1, 814.

[301] CONCILIUM OECUMENICUM VATICANUM II, Decretum de Oecumenismo *Unitatis Redintegratio 7*, *AAS* 57 (1965) 90-112, 97. tr. "All the faithful should remember that the more effort they make to live holier lives according to the Gospel, the better will they further Christian unity and put it into practice. For the closer their union with the Father, the Word, and the Spirit, the more deeply and easily will they be able to grow in mutual brotherly love". Quoted from VATICAN COUNCIL II, *Unitatis Redintegratio*: in *The Conciliar and Post Conciliar Documents* 1, 460.

The same document says in number 15 that the manifestation of this mystery of communion is actualised above all in the celebration of the Eucharist:

> Omnibus quoque notum est quanto cum amore Christiani orientales liturgica Sacra peragant, praesertim celebrationem eucharisticam, fontem vitae Ecclesiae et pignus futurae gloriae, qua fideles cum episcopo uniti accessum ad Deum Patrem habentes per Filium Verbum incarnatum, passum et glorificatum, in effusione Sancti Spiritus, communionem cum Sanctissima Trinitate consequuntur, «divinae consortes naturae» (2 Pt. 1, 4) effecti[302].

On the basis of the teachings of Vatican II, I am trying to explain the Altar as the symbolism of covenant and communion. The consecration of the Altar is the union of Christ and His members, the nuptials of Christ and His Bride, the Church. The sacrifice of this holy Altar will henceforth be the sacrifice of the whole Christ, Head and members[303]. In the prayer of dedication, in *Ordo Dedicationis Ecclesiae et Altaris,* we see the idea of communion expressed in relation to the Trinity: "*Sit locus intimae tecum communionis et pacis, ut qui corpora et sanguine Filii tui vescentur eius Spiritu imbuti, in tuo crescant amore*"[304].

In these lines of the prayer, we see the three Authors of our Salvation present and active. God the Father is placed in relation to the idea and reality of communion. The Son is in relation to the Sacrament of His Body and His Blood and the Holy Spirit is in relation to the animation of Charity. The Altar is contemplated as the foundation of communion with God, of the participation at the banquet of the Sacrament of body and blood of the Lord and the place of Charity[305].

In the same formula of dedication, there is reference to the Eucharistic table as the place of spiritual nourishment for the community. Therefore the whole is seen with reference to the community's spiritual growth, for that community gathered around the Altar of celebration, a visible sign of the invisible unanimity of hearts, is the true

---

[302] CONCILIUM OECUMENICUM VATICANUM II, Decretum de Oecumenismo *Unitatis Redintegratio 15, AAS* 57 (1965) 90-112, 101-102. tr. "Everyone also knows with what great love the Christians of the East celebrate the sacred liturgy, especially the eucharistic celebration, source of the Church's life and pledge of future glory, in which the faithful, united with their bishop, have access to God the Father through the Son, the Word made flesh, Who suffered and has been glorified, and so, in the outpouring of the Holy Spirit, they enter into communion with the most holy Trinity, being made 'sharers of the divine nature'". Quoted from VATICAN COUNCIL II, *Unitatis Redintegratio*, 465.
[303] M. J. BEHEN, «The Christian Altar», 427.
[304] *Ordo Dedicationis Ecclesiae et Altaris, Pontificale Romanum, Ex Decreto Sacrosancti Ecumenici Concili Vaticani II Instauratum Auctoritate Pauli PP. VI Promulgatum*, 102.
[305] G. FERRARO, *Cristo è l'Altare: Liturgia di dedicazione della chiesa e dell'Altare*, 261.

spiritual temple, built with living stones (1Pet 2, 5)[306]. Ferraro adds the formula stating that the Altar is dedicated to God, and it is the property of God with the sanctification of the Holy Spirit and with the sacrificial banquet of the Son of God where the faithful are nourished[307]. He insists that the idea of communion is outlined by St. Paul in relation to the sacrificial banquet of the Lord[308]. According to Ferraro, "The Altar is the place where converges all the life of the universal and local communities"[309].

In the same prayer of dedication, we see that the Altar is referred to as a source of unity and friendship where people gather as one; "*Sit fons unitatis Ecclesiae et fatrum concordiae ad qeum fideles tui una convenientes spiritum hauriant mutuae caritatis*"[310].

Ferraro comments this part of prayer by saying that from the sacrifice of Christ originates the unity of the people of God. This is already revealed in John 11, 51-52. In the prayer of Jesus, he asks the Father, "Holy Father, protect them in your name that you have given me, so that they may be one, as we are one". He affirms in John 17, 19, "that they may all be one. As you, Father, are in me and I am in you, may they also be in us, so that the world may believe that you have sent me". The Eucharistic sacrifice is the efficacious sign of the Church's unity around the Altar[311].

One of the Fathers of the Church, St. Clement in his work "Les Stromates" VII, 6, 31,8, says about the union of the faithful around the Altar, "*Ἔστι γοῦν τὸ παρ᾽ ἡμῖν θυσιατήριον ἐνταῦθα τὸ ἐπίγειον [τὸ] ἄθροισμα τῶν εὐχαῖς ἀνακειμένων, μίαν ὥπερ ἔχον φνωήν τὴν κοινήν καὶ μίαν γνώμην*"[312].

The same idea is affirmed in *Lumen Gentium 3* that in the Eucharist the unity of the faithful is represented and effected:

---

[306] M. C. IGNAZIO, *The Dedication of a Church and an Altar: A Theological Commentary*, 8.
[307] G. FERRARO, *Cristo è l'Altare: Liturgia di dedicatione della chiesa e dell'Altare*, 255.
[308] G. FERRARO, *Cristo è l'Altare: Liturgia di dedicatione della chiesa e dell'Altare*, 261.
[309] G. FERRARO, *Cristo è l'Altare: Liturgia di dedicatione della chiesa e dell'Altare*, 255.
[310] *Ordo Dedicationis Ecclesiae et Altaris, Pontificale Romanum, Ex Decreto Sacrosancti Ecumenici Concili Vaticani II Instauratum Auctoritate Pauli PP. VI Promulgatum*, 102.
[311] G. FERRARO, *Cristo è l'Altare: Liturgia di dedicatione della chiesa e dell'Altare*, 263-264.
[312] CLEMENT D'ALEXANDRIE, *Les Stromates: Stomate VII*, ed. A. Boulluec (Sources Chrétiennes 428), Paris, 1997, 116-118. tr. "Our Altar of sacrifice, the Altar, we have here below, is the earthly gathering of these devoted to prayer, those having one voice and being of one mind". Quoted from CLEMENT, «Carpets(Stomata)» in *Worship in the Early Church: An Anthology of Historical Sources Vol 1*, ed. & tr. L. J. Johnson, ed. & tr. L. J. Johnson, Liturgical Press, Minnesota 2009, 261-263, 262.

> Quoties sacrificium crucis, quo "Pascha nostrum immolatus est Christus" (1Cor 5,7), in Altari celebratur, opus nostrae redemptionis exercetur. Simul sacramento panis eucharistici repraesentatur et efficitur unitas fidelium, qui unum corpus in Christo constituunt (1Cor 10,17). Omnes homines ad hanc vocantur unionem cum Christo, qui est lux mundi, a quo procedimus, per quem vivimus, ad quem tendimus[313].

The same document *Lumen Gentium 11*, says, "*Porro corpore Christi in sacra synaxi refecti, unitatem Populi Dei, quae hoc augustissimo sacramento apte significatur et mirabiliter efficitur, modo concreto exhibent*"[314]. It adds that the community of Altar is united as a mystical body of Christ in *Lumen Gentium 26*; "*In quavis Altaris communitate, sub Episcopi sacro ministerio, exhibetur symbolum illius caritatis et unitatis Corporis mystici, sine qua non potest esse salus*"[315].

E. McDonald states that the Christian Altar is the concentration, the replica of the life of the whole community. It is the monument of their faith, the symbol of their hope, and the bond of their charity and communion[316]. Behen explains that at the Altar we find fellowship with Jesus Christ who was crucified, is risen, and is coming again[317].

G. S. Duncan in explaining the architecture of the Church states, "usually Corinthian columns hold a type of canopy, symbolizing the tent or tabernacle that sheltered the Ark of the Covenant in the wilderness"[318]. With the same idea Behen indicates that we are a people of the Altar like the children of Israel. "Our life as a community comes from the Altar. It is the source of our spiritual nationhood. Born on the Altar of the cross, the people of God renews itself day by day at the Altar"[319]. J.

---

[313] CONCILIUM OECUMENICUM VATICANUM II, Constitutio Dogmatica de Ecclesia *Lumen Gentium 3*, 6. tr. "As often as the sacrifice of the cross in which Christ our Passover was sacrificed, is celebrated on the Altar, the work of our redemption is carried on, and, in the sacrament of the eucharistic bread, the unity of all believers who form one body in Christ (8) is both expressed and brought about. All men are called to this union with Christ, who is the light of the world, from whom we go forth, through whom we live, and toward whom our whole life strains". Quoted from VATICAN COUNCIL II, *Lumen Gentium*, 351.

[314] CONCILIUM OECUMENICUM VATICANUM II, Constitutio Dogmatica de Ecclesia *Lumen Gentium 11*, 15. tr. "Strengthened in Holy Communion by the Body of Christ, they then manifest in a concrete way that unity of the people of God which is suitably signified and wondrously brought about by this most august sacrament". Quoted from VATICAN COUNCIL II, *Lumen Gentium*, 362.

[315] CONCILIUM OECUMENICUM VATICANUM II, Constitutio Dogmatica de Ecclesia *Lumen Gentium 26*, 31. tr. "In any community of the Altar, under the sacred ministry of the bishop, there is exhibited a symbol of that charity and unity of the mystical Body, without which there can be no salvation". Quoted from VATICAN COUNCIL II, *Lumen Gentium*, 381.

[316] E. MCDONALD, «The Consecration of the Altar», in *Orate Fratres 6* (1932/7) 308-312, 308.

[317] M. J. BEHEN, «The Christian Altar», 422.

[318] G. S. DUNCAN, *The Church Building as a Sacred Place: Beauty, Transcendence, and the Eternal*, 22.

[319] M. J. BEHEN, «The Christian Altar», 422.

Sister brings out the idea of Altar as the stone of covenant. "Altar is standing as the witness-stone of our covenant with God"[320]. We can conclude that the Altar is a symbol of covenant and communion bringing the people of God in union with God and within themselves.

## 2.2.2. THE SYMBOL OF TABLE

The Altar is essentially and rightfully what it was in the beginning: a table. It is only a table as it is the place where the gifts of bread and wine are deposited, changed to the body and blood of Christ by the holy words and are prepared for the nourishment of the souls. The congregation, as God's family, gathers around this table. Here the church becomes visible as the Church, that is, the community of the faithful. It was this way at the Last Supper: the Apostles gathered around the Lord at the holy table[321]. Pope Pius XII, in his Encyclical *Mediator Dei No. 62* affirms that the primitive form of the Altar is table form[322].

The Eucharist is a memorial instituted by our Lord for a remembrance of Himself. Jungmann says that a table is set and it is the Lord's table. For a long time Christian speech avoided, or at least refrained from using, the term for the Altar derived from pre-Christian religion and even today still employs the simple name *mensa* and Ἁγία τράπεζα[323]. The Altar is the table on which the priest commemorates and joins us to Christ's sacrifice. It is a most holy place on which mere bread and wine are placed, that become Christ's Body and Blood. An Altar on which the bloodless sacrifice of the Mass is presented is a most holy object. That is why we have rules about how to honour, preserve, and take care of the Altar[324]. Duncan says this to preserve the Altar as a holy table of the Church.

Christians have never had difficulty seeing their Altar as the Lord's Table. The sacrifice of the New Law was instituted against the background of a family supper. Our sacrifice is also a banquet. The difficulty has rather been to see nothing but the table, to

---

[320] J. SISTER, «The Altar is Christ», in *Orate Fratres 11* (1937/12) 552.
[321] J. JUNGMANN, «The New Altar», 36.
[322] PIUS XII, «Litterae encyclicae *Mediator Dei et hominum* (20 novembris 1947)», in *AAS* 39 (1947) 521-595.
[323] J. JUNGMANN, *The Mass of the Roman Rite: Its Origin and Development Vol I*, 178.
[324] G. S. DUNCAN, *The Church Building as a Sacred Place: Beauty, Transcendence, and the Eternal*, 20-21.

forget the Altar. The great Eucharistic heresy has been to deny the Altar in favour of the communion table. Therefore, Behen insists, "There must first be the sacrifice, then the sharing in the sacrifice; first the Altar, then the fruit of the Altar"[325]. Godfrey says that the Altar, accordingly, is the 'table of the Lord', but a table 'which is Christ' who is victim, sacrifice and Altar, a sacred table which is a sacramental sign of the covenant, a place of sacrificial as well as meal-encounter between man and God[326].

The aspect of the table comes from the meal that is shared on the Altar. The Altar is the table of the marriage-banquet, of the sacrificial meal of which Christ invites his family to participate[327]. The Christian Altar is by its very nature a table of Sacrifice and at the same time a table of the paschal banquet[328].

In *Ordo Dedicationis Ecclesiae et Altaris*, we see the prayer of dedication which asks for the grace of God so that the Altar which is consecrated in the Church may stand for ever as the Lord's table. The prayer of dedication is prayed as follows:

> Supplices ergo te, Domine, adprecamur: hoc Altare in domo Ecclesiae aedificatum caelesti sanctificatione perfunde, ut ara fiat Christi sacrificio in perpetuum dicata
> et mensa esista dominica, ubi plebs tua divino reficiatur convivo[329].

The second part contains the prayer of invocation of the Spirit, epicletic in structure and terminology: a supplication that the Lord will be present with the ineffable sanctifying power of his Spirit, in the Church and on the Altar; that they become a 'holy place' and a joyous "table" for the celebration of Christ's sacrifice, the paschal banquet[330]. In the rite of the dedication of the Church contains a prayer of dedication that has similar significance. The prayer asks God to send the Holy Spirit so that the Altar may be a ready table for the sacrifice of Christ:

---

[325] M. J. BEHEN, «The Christian Altar», 425-426.
[326] D. GODFREY, «The Place of Liturgical Worship», in *The Church and the Liturgy Vol 2*, 92-93.
[327] D. GODFREY, «The Place of Liturgical Worship», in *The Church and the Liturgy Vol 2*, 92.
[328] R. KELMENS, *The Meaning of the Sacramental Symbols: Answers to Todays Questions*, 146.
[329] *Ordo Dedicationis Ecclesiae et Altaris, Pontificale Romanum, Ex Decreto Sacrosancti Ecumenici Concili Vaticani II Instauratum Auctoritate Pauli PP. VI Promulgatum*, 101. tr. "Lord, we therefore stand before you in prayer. Bless this Altar built in the house of the Church, that it may ever be reserved for the sacrifice of Christ, and stand for ever as the Lord's table where your people will find nourishment and strength". Quoted from *Dedication of a Church and an Altar*, 81.
[330] M. C. IGNAZIO, *The Dedication of a Church and an Altar: A Theological Commentary*, 24.

> Supplices ergo te, Domine, adprecamur: dignare hanc ecclesiam et hoc Altare caelesti sanctificatione perfundere, ut locus sanctus semper esista et mensa fiat in perpetuum Christi sacrificio parata[331].

Ferraro says that in fact, Jesus instituted the Eucharist during the paschal banquet and invited believers to eat His body and blood (Mt 26, 26-28; Mk 14, 22-24; Lk 22, 19-20 & Jn 6, 56)[332]. St. Paul also refers to the Altar as the 'Table of the Lord'(1Cor 10, 21). The prayer proposed for the preparation for the Eucharistic celebration before Vatican II, also express the idea of Table of the Lord. The prayer attributed to St. Ambrose has the following expressions: *"Ad mensam dulcissimi convivii tui, pie Domine Iesu Christe, ege..... accedere vereor et contremisco"*[333].

With this table and this banquet in which the food is Jesus himself, the participants are given rest from the daily worries of the world as he said in Mathew 11, 28, "Come to me, all you that are weary and are carrying heavy burdens, and I will give you rest". From this nourishment the faithful obtain the strength for the pilgrimage of the world towards the heavenly homeland. We see Elia in 1Kings 19, 18, after having eaten and drunk the food and water given by God, walked for forty days and forty nights until he reached the mountain of God[334]. For the journey of life, the Altar as the table of the Lord bears the body and blood of Christ and is distributed to the faithful to strengthen them.

Ignazio in his theological explanation of the dedication rite says that during the rite of the dedication of the Altar, it has been honoured with incense. Now other signs follow so that it might efficaciously express its original function as a table of the Lord (1Cor 10, 21), around which happily sit the sons and daughters who share the table with Christ. The prayer of dedication of the Altar joyously proclaims this meaning: "Make it [this Altar] a table of joy, where the friends of Christ may hasten" (No. 48)[335].

---

[331] *Ordo Dedicationis Ecclesiae et Altaris, Pontificale Romanum, Ex Decreto Sacrosancti Ecumenici Concili Vaticani II Instauratum Auctoritate Pauli PP. VI Promulgatum*, 46. tr. "Lord, send your Spirit from heaven to make this Church an ever-holy place, and this Altar a ready table for the sacrifice of Christ". Quoted from *Dedication of a Church and an Altar*, 55.

[332] G. FERRARO, *Cristo è l'Altare: Liturgia di dedicatione della chiesa e dell'Altare*, 259.

[333] *Praeparatio ad Missam*, in Missale Romanum Ex Decreto Sacrosancti Oecumenici Concilii Vaticani II, Instauratum auctoritate Pauli PP.VI promulgatum, Ordo Missae, Typis Polyglottis Vaticanis, Romae 1969, lviii.

[334] G. FERRARO, *Cristo è l'Altare: Liturgia di dedicatione della chiesa e dell'Altare*, 260.

[335] M. C. IGNAZIO, *The Dedication of a Church and an Altar: A Theological Commentary*, 30.

The General Instruction of the Roman Missal clearly states that the Altar on which the Sacrifice of the Cross is made present under sacramental signs is also the table of the Lord.

> Altare, in quo sacrificium crucis sub signis sacramentalibus præsens efficitur, est etiam mensa Domini, ad quam participandam in Missa populus Dei convocatur; atque centrum gratiarum actionis, quæ per Eucharistiam perficitur[336].

Thus we can conclude that the Altar is the table of the Lord and we are called to share in his loving meal as a community around the Altar.

### 2.2.3. THE SYMBOL OF CHRIST

The Altar is Christ not because in those days the Holy Eucharist was reserved in the tabernacle on the Altar, but because by the anointing with chrism it became a symbol of Christ. It is the consecration of the Altar which identifies it with Christ, which clothes it with beauty and splendor, no matter how poor it may appear to the eye. In that solemn ceremony the Altar is treated as though it were a living person, in fact as the person of the Incarnate Word[337]. The Rite of Consecration of the Altar consists of three clearly-marked phases, the baptism of the Altar with water, the entombment of the relics, and the anointing with the holy oils. The theme of the rite has been called by a liturgist the 'Christification' of the Altar, which identifies of Christ with the Altar, symbolically[338].

St. Ambrose asks, in his work, "*De Sacramentis*" in Catechesis fifth Chapter II, 7, 'What is Christ's Altar unless the image of Christ's body?':

> Tamen propter sequential anima tue vel condition humana vel ecclesia videt se ab omnibus mundatam esse peccatis, dignam quae ad Altare Christi posit accedere – quid est enim Altare nisi forma corporis Christi? – videt sacramenta mirabilia et ait: Osculetur me ab osculis oris sui, hoc est, osculum mihi Christus infigat[339].

---

[336] *Institutio Generalis Missalis Romani No. 296*, in *Missale Romanum Ex Decreto Sacrosancti Oecumenici Concilii Vaticani II, Instauratum auctoritate Pauli PP.VI promulgatum Ioannis Pauli PP. II cura recognitum*, 68. tr. "The Altar on which the Sacrifice of the Cross is made present under sacramental signs is also the table of the Lord to which the People of God is called together to participate in the Mass, as well as the centre of the thanksgiving that is accomplished through the Eucharist". Quoted from *General Instruction of the Roman Missal: Liturgy Documentary Series 2*, 101.
[337] J. SISTER, «The Altar is Christ», 550.
[338] J. SISTER, «The Altar is Christ», 551.
[339] AMBROSIUS, «De Sacramentis», in *Des Sacraments Des Mysteres*, 90. tr. "Yet because what follows your soul or the human condition or the Church speaks, seeing itself purified from all sins and worthy of

The Decree which introduces the 'Rite for the Dedication of a Church and an Altar' says that the Altar of a Church is Christ himself. He is the priest, the victim and the Altar. "*Altare vero, quod plebs sancta circumdat ut sacrificium dominicum participet et caelesti reficiatur convivo, signum existit Christi, qui sacerdos, hostia, Altare est sui ipsius sacrifici*"[340].

The United States Conference of Catholic Bishops, in the document *Built of Living Stones number 57*, says that the Altar should be fixed, that is, with the base affixed to the floor and with a table or *mensa* made of natural stone, since it represents Christ Jesus, the living stone (1Pet 2, 4)[341]. There is always a symbolic identification of Altar with Christ, the rock (1Cor 10, 4), the cornerstone (1Pet 2, 7; Eph 2, 20), the living stone (1Pet 2, 4)[342]. The stone of the Altar is the sign of Christ. The prayer includes three Biblical texts from New Testament: 1Pet 2, 4-8; 1Cor 10, 1-4 & Jn 19, 34. These texts say the theological background of the stone and affirm that Christ is that Stone and the Altar is the sign of Christ[343].

*Ordo Dedicationis Ecclesiae et Altaris* brings out the Biblical symbolism of stone with the Altar and Christ: "*Iuxta traditum Ecclesiae morem et symbolum biblicum quod Altari inest, mensa Altaris fixi sit lapidea, et quidem ex lapide naturali*"[344]. The same is also insisted in the General Instruction of the Roman Missal 301[345].

In *Ordo Dedicationis Ecclesiae et Altaris*, the dedication prayers bring out the idea that the Altar is identified with the Christ who is on the cross from whose body flowed blood and water as a sign of sacraments; "*Hic expolitus lapis sit nobis Christi*

---

approaching Christ's Altar – for what is Christ's Altar unless the image of Christ's body? Seeing the wonderful sacraments, it says, 'Let him kiss me with the kisses of his mouth'(Cant 1:2), that is, 'let Christ kiss me'". Quoted from AMBROSE, «De Sacramentis (on the Sacraments)», 60.

[340] DECRETUM (Prot. No. CD 300/77), 5. tr. "The Altar of a Church, around which the holy people of God gather to take part in the Lord's sacrifice and to be refreshed at the heavenly meal, stands as a sign of Christ himself, who is the priest, victim, and the Altar of his own sacrifice". Quoted from *Dedication of a Church and an Altar*, 85.
[341] UNITED STATES CONFERENCE OF CATHOLIC BISHOPS, *Built of Living Stones (2000)*, 433.
[342] R. KELMENS, *The Meaning of the Sacramental Symbols: Answers to Todays Questions*, 145.
[343] G. FERRARO, *Cristo è l'Altare: Liturgia di dedicatione della chiesa e dell'Altare*, 256.
[344] *Ordo Dedicationis Ecclesiae et Altaris, Pontificale Romanum, Ex Decreto Sacrosancti Ecumenici Concili Vaticani II Instauratum Auctoritate Pauli PP. VI Promulgatum*, 85. tr. "In accordance with received custom in the Church and the Biblical symbolism connected with an Altar, the table of a fixed Altar should be of stone, indeed of natural stone". Quoted from *Dedication of a Church and an Altar*, 67.
[345] *Institutio Generalis Missalis Romani No. 301*, in *Missale Romanum Ex Decreto Sacrosancti Oecumenici Concilii Vaticani II, Instauratum auctoritate Pauli PP.VI promulgatum Ioannis Pauli PP. II cura recognitum*, 69.

*signum, e cuius percusso latere unda manavit et cruor, quibus Ecclesiae sunt condita sacramenta*"[346].

The person of Christ is first and fundamental sacrament of God in His humanity and from whom came the sacraments which are signified by the blood and the water flew from the His wounded side. Therefore, from the Altar which is the sign of Christ, springs the sacraments which sanctify and vivify the faithful and the Church[347].

In the Letter to the Hebrews 13, 10-12, the author states: "We have an Altar from which those who officiate in the tent have no right to eat. For the bodies of those animals whose blood is brought into the sanctuary by the high priest as a sacrifice for sin are burned outside the camp. Therefore Jesus also suffered outside the city gate in order to sanctify the people by his own blood". It indicates that this Altar is not just the Eucharistic table, but the Cross on which Christ was slain, through which we offer our prayers to God. St. Thomas Aquinas in his commentary on above verse says the Altar of Christ is his immolated body on the cross and this Altar is nothing but the same Cross of Christ. Later it means the Eucharistic table. "*Istud Altare vel est crux Christi in qua, Christus pro nobis immolatus est; vel ipse Christus, in quo et per quem preces nostras offerimus*"[348].

In the *Praenotanda 4* of *Ordo Dedicationis Ecclesiae et Altaris,* we see that the heading given is '*Altare Christi signum*', and the concluding line is '*Altare Christus est*'[349]. It brings out the idea that the Altar is Christ as follows:

> Ex eo quod apud Altare memorial Domini celebrator eiusque Corpus et Sanguis fidelibus praebetur, factum est ut Ecclesiae scriptores in Altari veluti signum ipsius Christi cernerent – unde illud invaluit: 'Altare Christus est'[350].

---

[346] *Ordo Dedicationis Ecclesiae et Altaris, Pontificale Romanum, Ex Decreto Sacrosancti Ecumenici Concili Vaticani II Instauratum Auctoritate Pauli PP. VI Promulgatum*, 102 -103. tr. "Make this Altar a sign of Christ from whose pierced side flowed blood and water, which ushered in the sacraments of the Church". Quoted from *Dedication of a Church and an Altar*, 81.

[347] G. FERRARO, «Il Mistero di Cristo nella liturgia della dedicazione», in *La Civilta Cattolica 133* (1986/3) 239-251, 246-248.

[348] THOMAE AQUINATIS, «In Epistolam ad Hebraeos», in *Divi Thomae Aquinatis Doctoris Angelici Ordinis Praedicatorum. Opera VII-VIII*, Venetiis, 1747, 407-584, 579.

[349] *Ordo Dedicationis Ecclesiae et Altaris, Pontificale Romanum, Ex Decreto Sacrosancti Ecumenici Concili Vaticani II Instauratum Auctoritate Pauli PP. VI Promulgatum*, 83.

[350] *Ordo Dedicationis Ecclesiae et Altaris, Pontificale Romanum, Ex Decreto Sacrosancti Ecumenici Concili Vaticani II Instauratum Auctoritate Pauli PP. VI Promulgatum*, 83. tr. "At the Altar the memorial of the Lord is celebrated and his body and blood given to the people. Therefore the Church's writers have seen in the Altar a sign of Christ himself. This is the basis for the saying: 'The Altar is Christ'". Quoted from *Dedication of a Church and an Altar*, 66.

The prayer of dedication addresses Christ as, "*Christo summon Pontifici atque Altari vivo*"[351]. Thus, we can conclude that the Altar is the symbol of Christ because of its centrality in the Eucharistic celebration and the actions that take place above the Altar.

## CONCLUSION TO THE SECOND CHAPTER

In the attempt to understand the gestures, veneration and symbolism centered on the Altar, I tried to bring out some important elements. As the Altar deserves the greatest attention and veneration in the Church, a Christian expresses his veneration through gestures and adornment. In the gestures, I have tried to explain the importance of incensing, kissing, bowing and genuflecting. Incense is a sign of prayers ascending to God so that God's mercy might descend on us. It is also a sign of abasement as it is totally consumed in the charcoal. Moreover it calls every Christian to be the incense and its essence is Christ.

In the gesture of Kissing, the presence of Christ is emphasized. It is a brotherly greeting and can also be a bridal kiss. Both bowing and genuflecting are the signs of veneration and reverence by humbling oneself before the divine presence. This gesture brings one to realize the greatness of God. The Altar is adorned because it is the symbol of Christ Himself. There is a general rule that any adornment should not interfere with the clear view of the Altar for the participants. By clothing the Altar, one is clothing Christ Himself. The Altar cloth symbolizes the linen in which the body of Christ was wrapped. It has much to teach for a Christian to remain pure and sinless. The Altar Cross is placed there to recall that the sacrifice that is offered on the Altar is the same sacrifice of the Cross. The Altar candles signify the light of Christ. The living flame of the candle is a symbol of the Risen Christ and a reminder for the people of their baptism. Therefore, electric lights should not substitute the candles which are the symbol of sacrifice.

The Altar flowers serve as a reminder of the gift of God. As the liturgy is life and loves life, it desires living flowers. Therefore, it is forbidden to use artificial flowers

---

[351] *Ordo Dedicationis Ecclesiae et Altaris, Pontificale Romanum, Ex Decreto Sacrosancti Ecumenici Concili Vaticani II Instauratum Auctoritate Pauli PP. VI Promulgatum*, 102.

of cheap materials. Flowers are also a symbol of virtue, man's transient life and sacrifice. At the same time, there should be moderation in decorating. When coming to symbolism of Altar, I limit myself with three aspects: Symbol of Covenant and Communion, Table and Christ.

The Altar is contemplated as the foundation of communion with God and among the faithful themselves. It is the place at which all the life converges in the universal and local communities. It is also a standing witness-stone of our covenant with God. Christians have never had difficulty seeing the Altar as the Lord's Table. This symbolism comes because of the meal that is shared on the Altar and moreover it was originally a dining table at the Last Supper. By anointing the Altar with Chrism, it becomes a symbol of Christ. There is also the image of stone connected with Christ and from the Altar, the sign of Christ, springs the sacraments. Thus, the gestures, veneration and symbolism with regard to the Altar have really profound meaning and not mere cultic observations.

**Crypt Church of St. Maria Goretti - Altar has remains of her body, Nettuno, Italy.**

# CHAPTER THREE
# THEOLOGICAL AND LITURGICAL UNDERSTANDING AND THEIR IMPLICATIONS

Just as the Eucharist is the centre of Christian worship, so the Altar is the ideal centre of the Church building: all leads to and all leads from the Altar. The Altar is the 'place of concentration' of the liturgical spirituality and the Christian piety[352]. In this chapter I would like to explore the deeper meaning behind the gestures, veneration and symbolism around Altar. It is really necessary to have the knowledge about these aspects as the celebrants and participants are encountering them every time they pray and celebrate liturgy. These may really enkindle every Christian to celebrate the liturgy and enhance people to appreciate the deeper insights in the liturgical settings and celebration of the liturgy.

## 3.1. THEOLOGICAL AND LITURGICAL UNDERSTANDING

The symbolism of the Altar is inexhaustible, as are the mysteries it celebrates. In this heading I try to explain the gestures, veneration and symbolism under three aspects which are in my opinion important aspects, namely: Christocentric Understanding, Ecclesiological Understanding and Sacrificial Understanding. The Altar is at the centre of the sacred space and the liturgy. It is already been shown in the second chapter that the Altar symbolizes Christ and Communion. In this heading, I extensively explore the gestures, symbolism and veneration and how they are Christological, ecclesiological and sacrificial.

### 3.1.1. CHRISTOCENTRIC UNDERSTANDING

The Altar which is made of stone represents Christ from the Biblical point of view. The Altar is made of natural stone because the Altar represents Christ, the rock, the corner stone (1 Cor 10, 4; Eph 2, 20; 1 Pet 2, 4)[353]. The relation exists between stone and the Altar, based on the texts of the Old Testament, and on the Pauline allegory, 'The rock was Christ' (1 Cor 10, 4) contributed to the general use of the stone Altar, and on

---

[352] M. G. BOYER, *The Liturgical Environment: What the Documents Say*, 47.
[353] J. B. O'CONNELL, *Church Building and Furnishing*, 133.

the other to formulation in the patristic age of the current prayer '*Altare Christus est*'[354]. Nicholas says that the Altar manifests Christ. It is anointed with the Holy Spirit (Ps 44, 31); the head of the whole Church (Col 1, 18); in him the life and glory of the saints lay hidden (Col 3, 3). It signifies the Cross on which Christ offered himself[355].

As early as the 6th century there was local legislation requiring Altars to be made of stone. The council of Epaon (France) in 517 decreed that only stone Altars may be anointed with chrism[356]. In 769 and 806 the Capitularies of Charlemagne forbade wooden Altars. In England and Spain, in the 11th century, there was synodal legislation requiring Altars to be of stone. This material was universally used by the 12th and 13th centuries. Finally, the General Rubrics of the Missal (17th century) and the rubrics of the Roman Pontifical ( 1598) prescribed stone for all Altars[357]. O'Connell says that the Altar table must consist of one single slab, unbroken, without parts, fractures or cervices, symbolizing the personal unity of Christ, its surface normally being smooth and polished[358].

The Altar, hallowed by a solemn rite, becomes a sacred thing, that it may more perfectly symbolize Christ; it acquires a certain spiritual power for the more perfect fulfilment of the chief act of the sacred liturgy[359]. Christ means the 'Anointed one', how then could the Altar become a fitting symbol of the Anointed One without having been anointed? Such considerations suggested the anointing of the Altar; but the rite also strove to repeat the actions of the patriarchs when they raised Altars to God, as did Jacob who "took the stone that he had put under his head, set it up as a memorial stone, and poured oil on top of it" (Gen 28, 18)[360]. The *praenotanda* itself clearly says that the anointing with chrism makes the Altar a symbol of Christ:

---

[354] M. C. IGNAZIO, *The Dedication of a Church and an Altar: A Theological Commentary*, 25.
[355] M. NICHOLAS, *Altars according to the Code of Canon Law*, 36.
[356] J. B. O'CONNELL, *Church Building and Furnishing*, 136.
[357] J. B. O'CONNELL, *Church Building and Furnishing*, 136.
[358] J. B. O'CONNELL, *Church Building and Furnishing*, 137.
[359] J. B. O'CONNELL, *Church Building and Furnishing*, 133.
[360] M. C. IGNAZIO, *The Dedication of a Church and an Altar: A Theological Commentary*, 26.

Chrismatis unction Altare fit symbolum Chrsiti, qui prae omnibus 'Unctus' est vocatur; nam Pater Spiritu Sancto unxit eum summumque constituit Sacerdotem, qui in Altari Corporis sui vitae sacrificium pro omnium salute offerret[361].

Duncan says that the Altar, which is anointed at the time of dedication, is much like Christ's body which was anointed before his death[362]. Ferraro brings out the liturgical Christology which is present in the 'Rite of the Dedication a Church and an Altar'. He analyzes the *praenotanda* and the euchological texts and highlights their Christological aspect[363]. We see in the consecration ceremony, Church and Altar are 'baptized' and 'confirmed' almost like human being; they are sprinkled on all sides with holy water and are anointed with holy oil; only after that is the first Eucharist is celebrated[364]. Clerck summarizes all the rites in the dedication as the Christian initiation rites. In the dedication rite, Altar is baptized, given confirmation by anointing and receives the body and blood of Christ at the Eucharistic Celebration[365].

The theme of the entire rite is the Christification of the Altar. Christ Himself taking up His abode in it identifies Himself with it. Thus the consecration is symbolically a sacrifice. Hence, the Altar, a gift to God representing the Church, is symbolically changed into Christ on behalf of the Church by consecration. This is brought about by a baptism of regeneration of the Altar to its new purpose, expressed by the use of water; and a consecration or Christification, infusing into the Altar Christ Himself and the fullness of the power of His Holy Spirit, expressed in the significance and unction with oil of catechumens and holy chrism[366].

There is a clear Christological aspect of Altar in the prayer of dedication of the Altar. The Altar is the visible sign of the mystery of Christ. "*Altare ac domum Quae*

---

[361] *Ordo Dedicationis Ecclesiae et Altaris, Pontificale Romanum, Ex Decreto Sacrosancti Ecumenici Concili Vaticani II Instauratum Auctoritate Pauli PP. VI Promulgatum*, 88. tr. "The anointing with chrism makes the Altar a symbol of Christ, who, before all others, is and is called 'The Anointed One'; for the Father anointed him with the Holy Spirit and constituted him the High priest so that on the Altar of his body he might offer sacrifice of his life for the salvation of all". Quoted from *Dedication of a Church and an Altar*, 70.
[362] G. S. DUNCAN, *The Church Building as a Sacred Place: Beauty, Transcendence, and the Eternal*, 20.
[363] G. FERRARO, «Cristo è l'Altare : Considerazioni sulla Tematica Cristologica nell '*Ordo Dedicationis Ecclesiae et Altaris*'», in *Notitiae 33* (1997) 72-86.
[364] J. JUNGMANN, *The Mass of the Roman Rite: Its Origin and Development Vol I*, 254.
[365] P. D. CLERCK, «Il Significato dell'Altare nei Rituali della Dedicazione», in *L'Altare*, ed., G. Boselli, Edizioni Qiqajon, Magnano 2003, 39-55, 45-46.
[366] E. MCDONALD, «The Consecration of the Altar», 309-310.

*nostro linimus minister Dominus sua virtute sanctificet Ut Christi et Ecclesiae mysterium Visibili exprimant signo*"[367]. The Altar is reffered to here as the mystery of Christ. In the prayer of the dedication of the Altar, Christ is mentioned as "*Christo, summon Pontifice atque Altari vivo*"[368].

If the Altar is the meeting place of God and man, then indeed Christ is the Altar. For in Christ not only do God and man meet, they are one. There can be no more perfect symbol of Jesus Christ than the Altar, for the Altar expresses perfectly His mission of mediator. Uniting man with God and man with man, He is the cornerstone of the New Dispensation. Christ is the Altar upon whom we lay our works and our prayers, uniting them with His eternal Sacrifice. Christ is the Altar around which our lives as Christians must always gravitate if they are to have value and significance for eternity[369]. The young cleric, about to be raised to the Order of sub-deacon, chooses Christ irrevocably by advancing to the Altar. On the Altar the monk lays the parchment which contains his religious profession. Before the Altar the consecrated virgin is espoused to Christ. The nuptial of God's children has always been held before the Altar. The Christian is a man of the Altar[370].

The incensing of the Altar is also derived from the Christological perspective. The Altar stands as a continuous prayer rising like perfumed smoke before the divine Majesty, to represent the mystical Christ, whose more worthy members, the martyrs, have become part and parcel of this Altar, members of it to represent the mystical Christ worshipping the ever glorious Trinity, inviting us to join in this worship by offering thereon the sacrificial incense of our Christian faith and Christian life[371]. The Altar is Christ, only for this motive Altar is incensed like Cross and it is also the unique object

---

[367] *Ordo Dedicationis Ecclesiae et Altaris, Pontificale Romanum, Ex Decreto Sacrosancti Ecumenici Concili Vaticani II Instauratum Auctoritate Pauli PP. VI Promulgatum*, 47. tr. "We now anoint this Altar and this building. May God in his power make them holy, visible signs of the mystery of Christ and his Church". Quoted from *Dedication of a Church and an Altar*, 36.

[368] *Ordo Dedicationis Ecclesiae et Altaris, Pontificale Romanum, Ex Decreto Sacrosancti Ecumenici Concili Vaticani II Instauratum Auctoritate Pauli PP. VI Promulgatum*, 102.

[369] M. J. BEHEN, «The Christian Altar», 425.

[370] M. J. BEHEN, «The Christian Altar», 422.

[371] E. MCDONALD, «The Consecration of the Altar», 361.

that is kissed by the Priest in the liturgy along with the book of Gospels. The two close expressions, Cross and *Evangelarium*, are the personification of the Altar[372].

The presence of Christ in the Altar is insisted by various Christian authors. St. Epiphanus, in his work against the heresy which said that the Mechisedech is superior to Christ, shows the transcendence of the priesthood of the Word made flesh;

> Πρῶτον μὲν ἑαυτὸν προσενέγκας, ἵνα λύσῃ θυσίαν παλαιᾶς διαθήκης, τὴν ἐντελεστέραν ζῶσαν ὑπὲρ παν· τὸν κόσμου ἱερουργήσας· αὐτός ἱερεῖον, αὐτός θῦμα, αὐτός ἱερεύς, αὐτός θυσιαστήριον, αὐτός Θεός, αὐτός ἄνθρωπος, αὐτός βασιλεύς, αὐτός ἀρχιερεύς, αὐτός πρόβατον, αὐτός ἀρνίον, τὰ πάντα ἐν πᾶσιν...[373]

Epiphanus emphasizes that Christ himself is the victim, Altar and the priest. We can derive a conclusion from that that as the Altar in which we celebrate the liturgical action Christ is present. St. Cyril of Alexandria, in his work on 'Adorotion and Cult to God in Spirit and Truth, in explaining the command given by God to Moses in Ex 20, 24, "You need make for me only an Altar of earth and sacrifice on it your burnt offerings and your offerings of wellbeing", writes as follows:

> Γήϊνον μὲν γὰρ ὀνομάζει θυσιαστήριον τὸν Ἐμμανουήλ· «Γέγονε γὰρ σὰρξ ὁ Λόγος.» Γῆ δὲ ἐκ γῆς ἡ σαρκός ἐστι φύσις. Ἐν Χριστῷ δὴ οὖν ἡ πᾶσα καρποφοία καί πᾶσα πορσαγωγή.[374]

Jesus is the Altar of earth, the Word incarnate. By this incarnation he also represents the humanity in him. He again insists the Immanuel aspect of the Altar saying:

> Μεμνη σόμεθα δέ καί τὸ θυσιαστήριον τὸ χρυσοῦν, καί αὐτὸ δέ τὸ σύνθτον καί λεπτὸν θυμίαμα Χριστὸν εἰρηκότες, καί αὐτὸν ἡμῖν τὸν Ἐμμανουήλ δι' ἀμφοῖν σημαίνεσθαι"[375].

---

[372] P. D. CLERCK, «Il Significato dell'Altare nei Rituali della Dedicazione», 49.
[373] EPIPHANIUS, *Epiphanus II: Ancoratus und Panarion*, ed. K. Holl, (Die Griechischen Christlichen Schritsteller), Akademie-Verlag, Berlin 1922, 330-331. tr. "Christ offered himself in order to abolish the sacrifices of the Old Covenant, sacrificing for the whole world a living victim, being himself the victim, himself the priest, himself the Altar, he himself God, himself man, he himself King, himself the high priest, he still sheep and lamb, became for us all in all". (Translated by me)
[374] CYRILLI ALEXANDRIAE, «De Adoratione in Spiritu et Veritate», in *Cyrilli Alexandriae Archiepiscopi Opera Quae Reperiri Potuerunt Omnia*, ed. J. P. Migne (PG 68), Thomus Primus, Paris 1864, 133-1126, 592-593. tr. "This Altar of earth, God calls him Emmanuel, because the Word was made flesh, and the nature of the flesh is soil taken from the earth. In Christ then there is every oblation and every access". (Translated by me)
[375] Cyrilli Alexandriae, «De Adoratione in Spiritu et Veritate», 648.

Cyril of Alexandria views the Altar as the continuous presence of the Word Incarnate and the Immanuel. Debuyst writes that the presence of Christ is a fraternal presence. The table of the Lord appears as directly rooted in a mystery of fraternal presence and a bearer of peace which the world cannot give, because the Altar is Christ himself[376]. The Altar is both a threshold and a table, because it corresponds to a precise function. At the same time, from the point of presence and from the Personal mystery of Christ it characterizes the presence of the Lord with dignity and integrity without flaw[377]. Clerck states that the presence is like a personal presence of Christ. He says that since it is the common understanding between humans to reserve the kiss to the people, when the priest kisses the Altar, all present in the liturgy can understand that the Altar is the one who summons them, the Lord Jesus[378].

G. Ferraro explains that Altar is named because of its analogy with Christ. Altar gets its name because of its conformity with Christ:

> Non è che cristo venga denominato Altare per analogia con gli Altari materiali delle nostre chiese; sono anzi questi che vengano denominati Altari per analogia con cristo, al quale per primo appartiene di essere Altare anche del nostro sacrificio come lo fu del suo[379].

Ferraro gives us a deeper theological understanding of the Altar. Christ is referred to the Altar sometimes to His body, sometimes to his humanity, namely body and soul. These two indications are substantially equal. The Altar of the sacrifice of Christ is the body of Christ, because in the ancient sacrifices, the Altar was the place on which the blood of the victim offered to God was poured, so also in the sacrifice of Christ, his blood which effused from his body and shed on his body. Now the body of Christ, which is the Altar of his Sacrifice, is his living body, that is, the body animated by the rational soul, whose human will joined with the will of God the Father in the offering of his self-sacrifice, in pouring out his blood. Body and soul form the humanity of Jesus, form his human nature. Now the human nature is to be personally assumed by

---

[376] F. DEBUYST, «L'Altare: Opera d'arte o Mistero di Presenza?», in *L'Altare*, ed., G. Boselli, Edizioni Qiqajon, Magnano 2003, 27-38, 29.
[377] F. DEBUYST, «L'Altare: Opera d'arte o Mistero di Presenza?», 30.
[378] P. D. CLERCK, «Il Significato dell'Altare nei Rituali della Dedicazione», 49.
[379] G. FERRARO, «Cristo è l'Altare : Considerazioni sulla Tematica Cristologica nell'*Ordo Dedicationis Ecclesiae et Altaris*'», 81. tr. "It is not that Christ is called the Altar by analogy with material Altars of our churches, indeed those who are called Altars because of the analogy with Christ, who is at first belongs to be Altar and also of our sacrifice as it was his". (Translated by me)

the Word of God, by the Son of God. And the Altar which expresses the human nature of Jesus is also inseparable from his divine nature. Thus, Jesus presents in himself the Altar for his sacrifice inasmuch as he is Human and Divine, inasmuch as he is Incarnate Word, inasmuch as he is the Son of God and the son of Mary[380].

From the above all we come to know the conformity of Altar with Christ and this Altar is given reverence and respect only because of the Christological aspects behind. As explained that the Altar is the mystical Christ present among the celebrating community, it is honored for the liturgical action that takes place on it.

### 3.1.2. ECCLESIOLOGICAL UNDERSTANDING

The Altar is the symbol of communion and unity. When we see the Old Testament, Forman says that the dedication of the Altar brought the people of Israel together as one community. He says that with the trials and tribulations of Egypt behind him, and having received the Ten Commandments, Moses faced a daunting challenge; how to forge the 12 tribes of the children of Israel into a nation. Despite the fact that they derived from common ancestors, shared the same experiences, and witnessed the same miracles, they had yet to be thoroughly enough united to enter into the Promised Land. It was Moses who had to achieve this unity, and as a first step toward that end he chose the dedication of the Altar[381]. We see that from the beginning, the Altar is a uniting force and even now whenever we celebrate the liturgy we gather around the Altar as one celebrating community.

In the commentary of the rite of dedication of the Altar, Ignazio says that if in the building dedicated to worship the Altar is Christ, then the stones holding up the walls are Christians (1 Pet 2, 5). As the Head was anointed with the Spirit, so are the members in the sacraments; as the Altar was anointed, so are the stones. The anointing of the new church's inner walls appears as ritual translation of this relationship, and as a second stage in the Christian initiation of the new ecclesial space[382].

---

[380] G. FERRARO, «Cristo è l'Altare : Considerazioni sulla Tematica Cristologica nell '*Ordo Dedicationis Ecclesiae et Altaris*'», 82-83.
[381] J. FORMAN, «Numerical symbolism in the dedication of the Altar», 52.
[382] M. C. IGNAZIO, *The Dedication of a Church and an Altar: A Theological Commentary*, 25-26.

The rite of the anointing begins at the Altar and continues with the walls; this more clearly builds to a climax, and manifests a deeper sense of the mysteries involved. Anointing of the members takes its meaning from the anointing of Christ the Head; in *signo*, anointing begins with the Altar, symbol of Christ, and proceeds to the side walls, symbols of Christians, stones of the Church. The Altar and the Church, marked with the same chrism, become an expressive sign of the mystery of Christ and his Church, that is, of 'the Anointed One' par excellence and his anointed people[383].

*Sacrosanctum Concilium* insists that the liturgical actions are not private functions. Whenever the liturgy is celebrated, it is the sacrament of unity and the action of the Whole Church.

> Actiones liturgicae non sunt actiones privatae, sed celebrationes Ecclesiae, quae est 'unitatis sacramentum', scilicet plebs sancta sub Episcopis adunata et ordinata. Quare ad universum Corpus Ecclesiae pertinent illudque manifestant et afficiunt; singula vero membra ipsius diverso modo, pro diversitate ordinum, munerum et actualis participationis, attingunt[384].

The Church is where the congregation meets; similarly, its Altar is the centre of the union between Christ and Church, where the oblation is unique and all comprehensive[385]. Godfrey says, "the *altiora principia* of the centrality of the Eucharist, and its end which is the unity of the Mystical body"[386]. The unity of the mystical body of Christ is realized by the liturgical action of the Altar. In a far deeper sense is the Altar the pivot of Christian history. The Christian Altar is not only a symbol of unity. It both symbolizes and affects the unity of the people of God, a unity far surpassing political or racial unity. When Christians could gather around a common Altar, they were indeed one people[387].

The ecclesial unity is the primary focus of the bishop's initial greetings that we see in the dedication of the Church:

---

[383] M. C. IGNAZIO, *The Dedication of a Church and an Altar: A Theological Commentary*, 27.
[384] CONCILIUM OECUMENICUM VATICANUM II, Constitutio de Sacra Liturgia *Sacrosanctum Concilium 26*. tr. "Liturgical services are not private functions, but are celebrations of the Church, which is the 'sacrament of unity', namely, the holy people united and ordered under their bishops. Therefore the liturgical services pertain to the whole body of the Church; they manifest it and have effects upon it". Quoted from VATICAN COUNCIL II, The Constitution on the Sacred Liturgy, *Sacrosanctum Concilium*, 30.
[385] M. C. IGNAZIO, *The Dedication of a Church and an Altar: A Theological Commentary*, 32.
[386] D. GODFREY, «The Place of Liturgical Worship», 92.
[387] M. J. BEHEN, «The Christian Altar», 422.

> His Sacris ritibus pia adsimus devotione, verbum Dei audientes cum fide, ut communitas nostra, ex uno baptismatis fonte renata, atque eadam mensa nutrita, in templum spiritale crescat et superno provehatur amore ad unum Altare congregatea[388].

The very purpose the Altar is designed and constructed is for the action of a community to encounter God[389]. Therefore, the ecclesial community is also a reason behind the Altar. The Altar through the Eucharist becomes holy for the faithful and for the whole Church. The Altar, at the celebration of the Eucharist, is the central point not only of the Church as a building but of the Church as the living assembly[390]. St. Clement says about the union of the faithful around the Altar, "*"Ἔστι γοῦν τὸ παρ᾽ ἡμῖν θυσιατήριον ἐνταῦθα τὸ ἐπίγειον [τὸ] ἄθροισμα τῶν εὐχαῖς ἀνακειμένων, μίαν ὥπερ ἔχον φνωὴν τὴν κοινὴν καὶ μίαν γνώμην*"[391]. The earthly gathering of the faithful with one mind and one voice around the Altar demonstrates the ecclesial unity. The Greek term, *κοινωνία*, expresses the unity that results from table fellowship with Christ and Christ's Church[392].

From the Altar, then, flows the spirituality of the assembly and of the individual members of the Church. "The Altar is the ideal center of the ecclesial edifice: all leads to and all leads from the Altar. The Altar is the 'place of concentration' of the purest liturgical spirituality and the most intense Christian piety"[393]. Frederic Debuyst narrates three examples from different periods where the celebration of the liturgy is around a small Altar. He quotes the celebrations of St. Augustine in the basilica of Hippo on a Sunday, Guardini celebrating mass in the chapel of university of Berlin and

---

[388] *Ordo Dedicationis Ecclesiae et Altaris, Pontificale Romanum, Ex Decreto Sacrosancti Ecumenici Concili Vaticani II Instauratum Auctoritate Pauli PP. VI Promulgatum*, 31-32. tr. "May we open our hearts and minds to receive his word with faith; May our fellowship, born in the one font of baptism and sustained at the table of the Lord, become the one temple of his Spirit, as we gather round his Altar in love". Quoted from *Dedication of a Church and an Altar*, 26.

[389] M. G. BOYER, *The Liturgical Environment: What the Documents Say*, The Liturgical Press, Collegeville 1990, 36.

[390] G. FERRARO, *Cristo è l'Altare: Liturgia di dedicatione della chiesa e dell'Altare*, Edizioni OCD, Roma 2004, 254.

[391] CLEMENT D'ALEXANDRIE, *Les Stromates: Stomate VII*, ed. A. Boulluec (Sources Chrétiennes 428), Paris 1997, 116-118. tr. "Our Altar of sacrifice, the Altar, we have here below, is the earthly gathering of these devoted to prayer, those having one voice and being of one mind". Quoted from CLEMENT, «Carpets(Stomata)», 262.

[392] P. H. JONES, «We are How we Worship: Corporate Worship as a Matrix for Christian Identity Formation», in *Worship 69* (1995/4) 346-360, 356.

[393] M. G. BOYER, *The Liturgical Environment: What the Documents Say*, 47.

a chapel built by Rudolf Schawarz, where people with the celebrant gathered around the small Altar to emphasize the communitarian aspect. The author says that the celebrating community is centered on the presence of Christ which is Altar[394]. The community is bound by the central gravitational pull of the Altar.

Carneiro writes in his article that the church building has Altar at its centre because Altar has the body of Christ. He says, *"Non ha più cuore, non ha più occhi, non ha più voce che per questo Altare in cui il corpo di Gesù brilla eternamente"*[395]. Behen compares the kissing of the Altar by the priest with the bridal kiss explaining that the Church through the priest kisses the groom Jesus symbolized in the Altar[396]. In the Second chapter, we already saw that the Altar cloth is the symbol of members of Christ. E. McDonald states that the Christian Altar is the concentration, the replica of the life of the whole community. It is the monument of their faith, the symbol of their hope, and the bond of their charity and communion[397].

S. Heid affirms that the Christian Altar is originally derived from the table at the Last Supper where they had a community meal. The first generations Christians had held the community meal ἀγάπη and the Eucharist on the same table. The original Christian Altar was a meal table formally and was an Altar functionally. Later, when the Eucharist was separated from the community meal, the table form was deliberately retained in memory of the Last Supper[398]. One can see the origin of the Altar as the table of the ecclesial community. Richter explains that the Altar as 'mystical Christ' must be the starting point and the center of the celebrating community[399]. From all the above arguments, we can conclude that the Altar, its symbolism, kissing and veneration has the ecclesiological understanding.

---

[394] F. DEBUYST, «L'Altare: Opera d'arte o Mistero di Presenza?», 31-36.
[395] A. R. CARNEIRO, «Realizzazioni di Altari in Francia e in Belgio», in *L'Altare*, ed., G. Boselli, Edizioni Qiqajon, Magnano 2003, 99-112, 109. tr. "It (the Church) no longer has the heart, has no more eyes, has no more voice for this reason (there is) Altar in which the body of Jesus shines eternally". (Translated by me)
[396] L. E. PHILIPS, *The Ritual Kiss in Early Christian Worship*, Groove Books Limited, Cambridge 1996, 5.
[397] E. MCDONALD, «The Consecration of the Altar», 308.
[398] S. HEID, «The Early Christian Altar – Lessons for Today», in *Sacred Liturgy: The Source and Summit of the Life and Mission of the Church*, ed. A. Reid, Ignatius Press, San Francisco 2014, 87-114, 91.
[399] K. RICHTER, «Comunita, Spazio Liturgico e Altare», in *L'Altare*, ed., G. Boselli, Edizioni Qiqajon, Magnano 2003, 181-200, 187.

### 3.1.3. SACRIFICIAL UNDERSTANDING

Sacrifice is a gift of gratitude and of homage that is presented to God. Sacrifice is the highest form of worship given to God and consists, according to the proper acceptation of the term, in making an oblation to God of some sensible thing by a lawfully appointed minister, in order to acknowledge, by the destruction or at least the change effected in the offering, the majesty and sovereign power of God and man's absolute dependence upon Him. Nature itself invariably inspired man with the idea that sacrifice is the essential and highest act of external religion. Worship, the response of the human creature to the Divine, is summed up in sacrifice[400].

From the world's foundation to the present moment, the existence of sacrifice may be more or less discovered amongst men throughout the earth, however widely separated from each other by almost immeasurable distances, or the interposition of barriers erected by nature. Nicholas states that wherever sacrifices were offered to God, the Altar was used as the place of sacrifice. The Altar, therefore, is as ancient as sacrifice and dates back to the origin of man[401]. Indeed Kevin insists in his work 'Models of the Eucharist', the Altar is the *locus* of where Christ's sacrifice is perpetuated[402].

D. Power in his book 'Eucharistic Mystery' emphasizes that there was no magisterial teaching on the Mass as sacrifice until the council of Trent[403]. Fernandes explains that the traditional teaching on the Holy Mass was vigorously stated by the Council of Trent, session XXII which discussed and came out with the Doctrine on the most Holy sacrifice of the Mass (September 17, 1562), against the protestants. He says that the Holy Mass was instituted by Our Lord during the Last Supper:

> In order to leave to His beloved Spouse the Church a visible sacrifice…by which the bloody sacrifice which He was once for all to accomplish on the Cross would be represented, its memory perpetuated until the end of the world and its salutary power applied for the forgiveness of sins… He offered His body and blood under the species of bread and wine to God the Father, and, under the same signs gave them to partake of to the disciples…[404]

---

[400] E. UNDERHILL, *Worship*, Harper & Brothers Publishers, New York 1937, 47.
[401] M. NICHOLAS, *Altars according to the Code of Canon Law*, 1.
[402] W. I. KEVIN, *Models of the Eucharist*, 236.
[403] D. POWER, *The Eucharistic Mystery: Revitalizing the Tradition*, Crossroads, New York 1994, 248.
[404] C. C. FERNANDES, *The Eucharist: the Paschal Mystery and the New Covenant*, Theological Publications in India, Bangalore, 1985, 15.

The Eucharist is and always was a ritual meal; it was intended to be a meal in which all the faithful share. The concept of sacrifice answers the question, 'what do we mean by what we are doing?' This meal proclaims the saving death of the Lord, the sacrificial act which reconciled man and God[405]. Kevin states that by its very nature the Altar emphasizes the sacrificial nature of the Eucharist[406]. Enrico Mazza adds that the Altar is first of all a table and when the concept, the Supper of the Lord is a sacrifice, is emphasized then the table of the Lord is understood as Altar. The theology that interpreted the Eucharist as Sacrifice is projected on the table of celebration and from that moment the table of the Lord became Altar[407].

Whenever we approach the Altar we are reminded of the command of our Lord Jesus 'Do this in memory of me'. Leon Dufour emphasizes how the Lord's command 'Do this in memory of me', refers not only to the enactment of the supper but more importantly to living our lives in obedience to Christ and in imitation of his example of what it means to give our lives in self-surrender and self-sacrifice[408]. Pauline challenge to "offer your bodies as a sacrifice..." (Rom 12, 1) calls each one of us to a far wider sense from a cultic sacrifice. Eucharist is the sacrifice of Christ is clear; that his sacrifice should be imitated and lived out by us in lives of self-transcendence, self-sacrifice, and service should be equally clear[409].

The United States Conference of Catholic Bishops, in the document *Built of Living Stones number 58*, says that the shape and size should reflect the nature of the Altar as the place of sacrifice and the table around which Christ gathers the community to nourish them[410]. The Church prolongs the priestly mission of Jesus Christ mainly by means of the sacred liturgy. *Mediator Dei* says that the Church does this priestly mission in the first place at the Altar where constantly the sacrifice of the cross is represented.

---

[405] T. GUZIE, *Jesus and the Eucharist*, Leominster, Gracewing, 1995, 146.
[406] W. I. KEVIN, *Models of the Eucharist*, 207.
[407] E. MAZZA, «Tavola e Altare: Due Modi non Alternativi per Designare un Oggetto Liturgico», in *L'Altare*, ed., G. Boselli, Edizioni Qiqajon, Magnano 2003, 55-81, 58.
[408] W. I. KEVIN, *Models of the Eucharist*, 235.
[409] W. I. KEVIN, *Models of the Eucharist*, 235.
[410] UNITED STATES CONFERENCE OF CATHOLIC BISHOPS, *Built of Living Stones: Art, Architecture, and Worship*, 433-434.

> Ecclesia igitur, accepto a Conditore suo mandato fideliter obtemperans, sacerdotale Iesu Christi munus imprimis per sacram Liturgiam pergit. Idque facit primario loco ad Altaria, ubi Crucis sacrificium perpetuo repraesentatur et, sola offerendi ratione diversa, renovatur[411].

In the rite of the dedication of the Altar, the *praenotanda* explains the use of incense and it connection with the sacrifice of Christ it represents:

> Incensum super Altare comburitur ut significetur sacrificium Christi, quod ibi in mystreio perpetuator, ad Deum ascendere in odorem suavitatis, sed et ut exprimatur fidelium orations placabiles gratasque usque ad thronum Dei pervenire[412].

The Roman Ritual '*De Benedictionibus*' gives a perfect explanation of the use of the Cross in the liturgy and Christian faithful and it explains the deeper meaning of its usage saying:

> Inter sanctas imagines, 'figura pretiosae et vivificae Crucis' principem obtinet locum, quipped quae symbolum sit totius paschalis mysterii. Nulla christianorm plebe carior est imago, nulla antiquor. Christi passio eiusque de morte triumphus per sanctam Crucem repraesentatur simulque, ut sancti Patres docuerunt, secundus idemque gloriosus nuntiatur eius adventus[413].

The United States Conference of Catholic Bishops affirms that the central image of Christianity is the Cross, calling to mind the passion, resurrection, and Christ's final coming in glory[414]. GIRM 296 brings out the sacrificial aspect of the Altar saying;

> Altare, in quo sacrificium crucis sub signis sacramentalibus præsens efficitur, est etiam mensa Domini, ad quam participandam in Missa populus Dei convocatur; atque centrum gratiarum actionis, quæ per Eucharistiam perficitur[415].

---

[411] Pius XII, «Litterae encyclicae *Mediator Dei et hominum* (20 novembris 1947)», 522.

[412] *Ordo Dedicationis Ecclesiae et Altaris, Pontificale Romanum, Ex Decreto Sacrosancti Ecumenici Concili Vaticani II Instauratum Auctoritate Pauli PP. VI Promulgatum*, 88. tr. "Incense is burned on the Altar to signify that Christ's sacrifice, there perpetuated in the mystery, ascends to God as an odor of sweetness and also to signify that the people's prayers rise up pleasing and acceptable, reaching the throne of God". Quoted from *Dedication of a Church and an Altar*, 70.

[413] *Rituale Romanum Ex Decreto Sanrosancti Oecumenici Concili Vaticani II Instauratum Auctoritate Ioannis Pauli II Promulgatum: De Benedictionibus*, Typis Polyglottis Vaticanis, Romae 1984, 364. tr. "Of all the sacred images, the 'figure of the precious, life-giving cross of Christ' is pre-eminent, because it is the symbol of the entire paschal mystery. The cross is the image most cherished by the Christian people and the most ancient: it represents Christ's suffering and Victory at the same time, as the Fathers of the Church have taught, it points to his Second coming". Quoted from United States Conference of Catholic Bishops, *Built of Living Stones: Art, Architecture, and Worship*, 489.

[414] United States Conference of Catholic Bishops, *Built of Living Stones: Art, Architecture, and Worship*, 451.

[415] *Institutio Generalis Missalis Romani No. 296*, in *Missale Romanum Ex Decreto Sacrosancti Oecumenici Concilii Vaticani II, Instauratum auctoritate Pauli PP.VI promulgatum Ioannis Pauli PP. II cura recognitum*, 65.

Whenever we celebrate the Eucharistic celebration, we make present the sacrifice of Cross under sacramental signs. The Altar receives its significance only from the liturgical action that takes place on it. It receives it authentic theological finality only from the great Eucharistic prayer. The sacrifice of Jesus it commemorates makes the Altar exist[416]. McKenna states that a thanksgiving over bread and wine is the form Christians use to commemorate Christ's suffering and death[417].

In the rite of the dedication of the Altar we see the following prayer which say that through the Altar we offer everlasting sacrifice of praise.

> Sit centrum nostrae laudis et gratiarum actionis, donec as aeterna tabenacula
> iubilantes perveniamus, ubi cum Christo, summon Pontifice atque Altari
> vivo, tibi perennis laudis sacrificium offeramus.[418]

The Altar is presented here as the centre of the prayer in variety of its forms: the praise, thanksgiving and sacrifice. Ferraro says that Christ is the only victim worthy of God. As the sacrifice makes the Altar exist, the Christ, who is the victim and the perfect sacrifice, is also the Altar, the only Altar of God. In the Incarnate Word takes place the encounter of God with humanity. Christ is the true Altar because he is the God-Man and the perfect Sacrifice. Every place, in which this mediation is accomplished between God and men, participates of Christ and his sacrifice may be truly configured to Christ Altar[419].

Carneiro states that the Altar is an explosion of joy, abstract forms and materials. It bursts from the ground towards heaven. It symbolizes Incarnation and resurrection. It is a haven of peace and it shows us the suffering but also its fulfillment, everlasting life[420]. It is not the faithful become the contemporaries of Jesus in the

---

[416] A. GERHARDS, «Teologia dell'Altare», in *L'Altare*, ed., G. Boselli, Edizioni Qiqajon, Magnano 2003, 213-232, 228.
[417] J. H. MCKENNA, «Eucharist and Sacrifice : an Overview», in *Worship 76* (2002/5) 386-402, 390.
[418] *Ordo Dedicationis Ecclesiae et Altaris, Pontificale Romanum, Ex Decreto Sacrosancti Ecumenici Concili Vaticani II Instauratum Auctoritate Pauli PP. VI Promulgatum*, 102. tr. "Make it the centre of our praise and thanksgiving until we arrive at the eternal tabernacle, where, together with Christ, high priest and living Altar, we will offer you an everlasting sacrifice of praise". Quoted from *Dedication of a Church and an Altar*, 81.
[419] G. FERRARO, «Cristo è l'Altare : Considerazioni sulla Tematica Cristologica nell 'Ordo Dedicationis Ecclesiae et Altaris'», 81.
[420] A. R. CARNEIRO, «Realizzazioni di Altari in Francia e in Belgio», 109.

Eucharistic celebration. But Jesus sacrifices himself in every Eucharistic sacrifice. So the Altar is called the Altar of Sacrifice[421].

## 3.2. IMPLICATIONS FOR TODAY

In this topic we are going to see the practical implications from what we have explored until now for the betterment of the liturgical celebration and of our daily Christian life. Liturgical implications give some guidelines for the better celebration and arrangement. Pastoral implications are the life messages that we derive from the gestures, veneration and symbolism around the Altar and we can put them into practice. Finally, I attempt to give some guidelines and proposals for the liturgy and Christian life.

### 3.2.1. LITURGICAL IMPLICATIONS

Behen states about the lack of appreciation on the part of modern generation for the signs and symbols that are used in the liturgy. He explains that the faithful are not ready to find the many signs in her worship when the Church makes a solemn celebration of the consecration of the Altar. An age impatient with symbolism has forgotten or ignored these gestures of the Holy Church. However, an understanding and appreciation of them will make us approach the Altar with renewed devotion[422].

A few basic rules given by Edward McDonald:

> (i) The Altar should first of all and unmistakably be a table; ornate but never losing the form of a table;
> (ii) The Altar should stand out alone and free from everything round about it;
> (iii) Nothing should ever be placed upon it or even near it which is not a holy object connected closely with the holy sacrifice;
> (iv) It should be kept spotless and tastefully and richly adorned with those vestitures prescribed by liturgical law for the different functions performed thereat;
> (v) it should be treated with the greatest of respect and reverence, whether the holy Sacrament is kept there or not, and no one should be allowed to attend it or even touch it without authorization to do so. In short, it is to be treated as though it were a living person, and not merely a living person, but as the Person of the Incarnate Son of God[423].

---

[421] A. GERHARDS, «Teologia dell'Altare», 217.
[422] M. J. BEHEN, «The Christian Altar», 427.
[423] E. MCDONALD, «The Consecration of the Altar», in *Orate Fratres 6* (1932/9) 410-415, 415.

Duncan insists that the liturgico-sacramental elements should be designed in such a way that people understand that they are holy objects, and not to be taken lightly[424]. He further notes that many of the Altars we have recently built do not harmonize with the meaning of the liturgy, nor do they live up to the standard set by the past. Some of the features, such as, an open table for a freestanding Altar, crude or cheap materials, an impermanent aesthetic element do not adequately symbolize the Altar. The size and scale of the Altar must be generous enough to be seen by all of the faithful and viewd as prominent within the church. It should clearly be the most important element in the church and therefore designed and constructed out of the finest materials such as marble. The design of the Altar should be such that it portrays the theological truths we wish to express[425].

All that is done in the liturgy is to indicate the epiphanous character of the liturgy. Everything matters from arrangements to lighting, sights, sounds and silences, movements, gesture and posture, and every word that proceeds from the mouth of the celebrant[426].

About the gestures of the celebrant, Church insists that the celebrant's gestures function as signs; they are meant to reveal Christ's presence. They will be effective only to the degree that they are motivated directly by an inner vision and the contemplation of mystery. Careful observance of rubrics, necessary though it is, is not enough here. The *Consilium* says:

> How can gestures that have become mechanical from habit, sloppy from routine, half-hearted from apathy still function as signs of the work of salvation? The Roman Ritual in one text from four and a half centuries ago demanded gestures of celebrants that by their dignity and gravity would serve as an effective message for the faithful, 'making them attentive and lifting them up to the contemplation of heavenly things'. Should the celebrants who handle, so to speak, the realities of the new and everlasting covenant be exempt from the same basic preparation?[427]

---

[424] G. S. DUNCAN, *The Church Building as a Sacred Place: Beauty, Transcendence, and the Eternal*, 20.
[425] G. S. DUNCAN, *The Church Building as a Sacred Place: Beauty, Transcendence, and the Eternal*, 20-21.
[426] D. B. BATCHELDER, «Holy God, Dangerous Liturgy: Preparing the Assembly for Transforming Encounter», in *Worship 79* (2005/4) 290-303, 295.
[427] CONSILIUM, «*Des gestes qui revelent,* on gentures in the Liturgy (January 1968)», in *Documents on the Liturgy 1963 – 1979, Conciliar, Papal, and Curial Texts*, The Liturgical Press, Minnesota 1982, 146-147, 146.

The Church admonishes the celebrant to observe the gestures according to the rubrics and with real devotion. The *Consilium* enlists saying: "these are things that must be learned: how to stand erect, bow, genuflect; how to bend over to kiss the Altar; how to make the sign of the cross over the offerings or trace it over the offerings or the congregation; how to raise the arms, extend the hands, join the fingers, etc."[428].

Gregory Dix once mentioned about his Wesleyan grandmother, when there was no *Altar versus populum*. She imagined seeing from the backside that the priest had a crab on the Altar and all his fiddling around with his back to the people was to prevent the crab from crawling off[429]. Now the priest is facing the people and the people see the gestures of the priest and the sacred action on the Altar. Therefore, the priest should very carefully perform his role without leaving the essential gestures.

To be graceful yet remain simple and unstudied, liturgical gestures demand at least a minimum of preparation and care. They also require at least a little time. Haste leaves no room at all for beauty. Liturgical gestures have to be performed unhurriedly and be of a measure suited to the gathered assembly, to which they are a revelation of the realities of the kingdom. The celebrant himself is a sign of Christ; he bears witness to Christ and the Church only to the degree that his bearing, his gestures, and his words allow his inner contemplation to show through[430]. So the gestures of the celebrant should be graceful, with proper preparation and not done in haste. The gestures around the Altar emphasize the presence of Christ and the humility and veneration towards the Altar. The ordained minister should not omit any specific manual acts during the Liturgy. The greatest care should be there during the liturgy not only how it sounds but also how it looks[431]. As we have seen the gestures and veneration with regard to the Altar and their importance, we can conclude that the people who really live by the liturgy will come to learn that the bodily movements, the actions, and the material objects which it employs are all the highest significances. It offers great opportunities of expression, of knowledge, and of spiritual experience; it is emancipating in its action,

---

[428] CONSILIUM, «*Des gestes qui revelent,* on gentures in the Liturgy (January 1968)», 146.
[429] G. DIX, *Shape of the Liturgy*, Dacre Press, Westminster 1945, 145.
[430] CONSILIUM, «*Des gestes qui revelent,* on gentures in the Liturgy (January 1968)», 146.
[431] D. GRAY, «Hands and Hocus-Pocus : The Manual Acts in the Eucharistic Prayer», in *Worship 69* (1995/4) 306-313, 313.

and capable of presenting a truth far more strongly and convincingly than can the mere word of mouth[432].

Prayerful and committed participation of the priest is very much necessary. Louis Bouyer says in his book 'Liturgy revived':

> The liturgy is not a kind of new trick, to be used just as any other pastoral device, to galvanize artificially the lives of the faithful. Those who are to make people live by it are to be the first to do it for themselves. We cannot be the priests of a religion of which we are not truly the faithful[433].

Therefore, the priests are called to faithfully observe the liturgical norms so that the people may take part in the liturgical celebrations actively by keeping the priest as their model. Napier highlighting the recommendation of the National Liturgical Commission of England and Wales in 'Pastoral Directory for Church Building', states that the celebration facing the people permits them to see the sacred action better, improves their dialogue with the celebrant and clearly indicates the unity of priest and people in the one celebration[434]. When people can see the sacred action, gestures and Altar arrangements better, they feel the need of participating actively. Hovda explains that the appearance and the gestures should also be upright. "In liturgical action, let any baptized, ordained celebrant and the concelebrants assess their participation including the way it looks"[435].

### 3.2.2. PASTORAL IMPLICATIONS

In the pastoral implications we try to see the implications that we derive from the gestures, veneration and symbolism for the daily lives of the faith community and the individual Christian. The ritual actions that follow the prayer of dedication of the Altar, such as, the anointing, the incensing, and the lighting of the Altar, are described in such a way as to highlight the dignity of both the Christian assembly and the Altar around which it is gathered. Thus, incense honors both Altar and the assembly. The

---

[432] R. GUARDINI, *The Church and the Catholic and the Spirit of Liturgy*, tr. A. Lane, Sheed & ward, New York 1940, 167.
[433] L. BOUYER, *The Liturgy Revived*, Darton Longman & Todd, London 1965, 107.
[434] C. NAPIER, «Altar in Contemporary Church», 628.
[435] R. W. HOVDA, *Strong, Loving and Wise : Presiding in Liturgy*, The Liturgical Press, Collegeville 1976, ix.

people of God are incensed because they are the living temple in which each faithful member is a spiritual Altar[436]. According to Boyer:

> In the future whenever the incense is used, it will not only recall the dedication of the Altar but the dedication of every individual baptized person who forms the assembly of believers. When the Altar is incensed, so are all the ministers and all the people incensed[437].

Moreover, he adds stating that when Altar is incensed, the Christian is remained that he or she is a gift of pleasing fragrance to God and a living sacrifice of praise. Each person is a temple of God wherein spiritual worship is offered[438].

In the Rite of the Dedication of the Church, the symbols of smoke and light are powerful allusions to the sacredness of the created space as well as the Christian call to holiness[439]. Therefore, due catechism should be given to the faithful about these rites and their inner meanings.

The Order of the Dedication of a Church and an Altar clarifies in the *praenotanda 5* that: "*Sua ipsius natura Altare uni Deo dicatur, nam sacrificium euchristicum uni Deo offertur. Hoc sensu intellegi debet consuetudo Ecclesiae dicandi Altaria Deo in hohorem Sancrorum*"[440]. An Altar is not dedicated to any of the martyrs, but to the God of Martyrs. This should be made clear to the people. The rite of the dedication of the Altar carefully adds in its instruction pastoral preparation for the dedication of the Altar, so that the Altar is properly respected:

> Fideles non solum tempestive certiores fiant de novi Altaris dedication, sed etiam opportune praeparentur ut actuose ritui intersint. Ideo, quid singuli ritus significant et quomodo peragantur erudiantur oportet. Ad quam impertiendam catechesim usui esse possunt quae supra dicta sunt de Altaris natura ac dignitate et de rituum sensu ac vi. Ita fideles recto ac debito erga Altare imbuentur amore[441].

---

[436] S. S. WILBRICHT, «An Ecclesiological Interpretation of the Rite of Church Dedication», in *Worship 80* (2006/4) 326-346, 337.
[437] M. G. BOYER, *The Liturgical Environment: What the Documents Say*, 44.
[438] M. G. BOYER, *The Liturgical Environment: What the Documents Say*, 48.
[439] S. S. WILBRICHT, «An Ecclesiological Interpretation of the Rite of Church Dedication», 342.
[440] *Ordo Dedicationis Ecclesiae et Altaris, Pontificale Romanum, Ex Decreto Sacrosancti Ecumenici Concili Vaticani II Instauratum Auctoritate Pauli PP. VI Promulgatum*, 84. tr. "The Altar is of its very nature dedicated to the one God, for the Eucharistic sacrifice is offered to the one God. This is the sense in which the Church's nature of dedicating the Altars to God in honor of the saints must be understood". Quoted from *Dedication of a Church and an Altar*, 68.
[441] *Ordo Dedicationis Ecclesiae et Altaris, Pontificale Romanum, Ex Decreto Sacrosancti Ecumenici Concili Vaticani II Instauratum Auctoritate Pauli PP. VI Promulgatum*, 89. tr. "The people are to be informed in good time about the dedication of a new Altar and they are to be properly prepared to take an

Behen clearly brings out the interrelation between three important aspects: the liturgical celebration on the Altar, the daily sacrifice of Christians for the Word of God and their eschatological fulfillment on the heavenly Altar. Christ is the Altar in heaven as well as on earth. "We have a High Priest who has taken his seat at the right hand of the throne of Majesty in the heavens, a minister of the Holies" (Heb 8, 1). Upon the golden Altar of heaven are offered the prayers of all the saints. The relics of the martyrs in the Altar of heaven are not dead bones, but "the souls of those who had been slain for the word of God" (Rev 6, 9)[442].

> The Altar of heaven is still a building. The number of those who are to be slain for the word of God is not yet complete. The Body of Christ, who is the Altar, is growing, until the number of the elect is complete. Every day at the Altar here on earth we look into the past and see our liturgy to be the culmination of man's efforts to offer sacrifice since the beginning of time. But we also look forward to the bright day of eternity and know that our liturgy is one with the worship of the saints in heaven. Our Altar on earth is one with the Altar in heaven. Our Altar is the meeting of heaven and earth. Here at the Altar our worship is joined with the worship of heaven, for both in heaven and on earth, the Altar is Christ[443].

Pope Pius XII in his encyclical *Mediator Dei No. 119*, exhorts that Christian faithful should approach the Altar offering themselves and those who are in their care. He admonishes the husbands and wives to get nourished on the Altar and bring up the children conformed to the mind and heart of Jesus:

> Excitate, Venerabiles Fratres, in eorum animis, qui vestris demandati sunt curis, studiosam ac veluti inexplebilem Iesu Christi famem; vobis magistris, Altaria pueris iuvenibusque stipentur, qui sese, innocentiam suam, suamque actuosam navitatem Divino offerant Redemptori ; frequentes accedant coniuges, qui ad sacram mensam enutriti, inde sumant ut subolem sibi creditam Iesu Christi sensibus eiusque caritate conforment[444].

The rite of the dedication of the Altar clearly brings out the idea that the Christian faithful are the spiritual Altars. "*Cum Christus, Caput et Magister, verum sit Altare, membra quoque ac discipuli Altaris sunt spiritalia, in quibus sacrificium vitae*

---

active part in the rite. Accordingly, they should be taught what each rite means and how it is carried out. For the purpose of giving this instruction, use may be made of what has been said earlier about the nature and dignity of an Altar and the meaning and import of the rite. In this way the rightful love that is owed to the Altar". Quoted from *Dedication of a Church and an Altar*, 72.

[442] M. J. BEHEN, «The Christian Altar», 428.
[443] M. J. BEHEN, «The Christian Altar», 428.
[444] PIUS XII, «Litterae encyclicae *Mediator Dei et hominum* (20 novembris 1947)», 565.

*sancte peractae Deo offertur*"[445]. Pope Gregory the Great also brings out the same idea in his homily on Ezekiel saying: *"Quid est tempulum, nisi fidelis populous?..... Et quid est Altare Dei, nisi mens bene viventium?.... Recte igitur est Altare Dei, nisi mens bene dicitur, ubi ex maerore compunctionis ignis ardet et caro consumitur"*[446].

When we see the Altar lights and clothing the following implications can be derived for the daily lives of the faithful. The festive lighting of the Altar reminds the Christian of the light of Christ received in baptism. Every time Altar is used, the candles near it are enkindled. The Christian is to 'keep the flame of faith alive' in his or her heart[447]. The clothing of the Altar in a white cloth echoes the garment of the new creation of baptism. In baptism the Christian, who has been 'clothed….in Christ', is instructed to bring his or her baptismal garment 'unstained to the judgment seat of Our Lord Jesus Christ' so that he or she 'may have everlasting life'[448]. Just as the linen only arrives at its dazzling whiteness after lengthy processing, the members of Christ endure the manifold sufferings and trials of this life on earth before they attain to glory in heaven[449]. Behen states that the faithful Christian lives in the shadow of the Altar. From birth to death, we are continually gravitating towards the Altar. The Christian is a man of the Altar[450].

Romano Guardini explains about double Altar saying, "the two Altars, the one without and the one within, belong inseparably together. The visible Altar at the heart of the Church is but the external representation of the Altar at the centre of the human breast, which is God's temple, of which the Church with its walls and arches is but the expression and figure"[451]. The Christian Altar is the center of Catholic parochial life and

---

[445] *Ordo Dedicationis Ecclesiae et Altaris, Pontificale Romanum, Ex Decreto Sacrosancti Ecumenici Concili Vaticani II Instauratum Auctoritate Pauli PP. VI Promulgatum*, 82. tr. "Since Christ, Head and Teacher, is the true Altar, his members and disciples are also spiritual Altars on which the sacrifice of a holy life is offered to God". Quoted from *Dedication of a Church and an Altar*, 65.

[446] GREGORII MAGNI, *Homiliae in Hiezechielem*, ed. M. Adriaen, Città Nuova Editrice, Roma 1993, 286-287. tr. "What is temple if not the faithful people? ... And what is that the Altar of God if not the soul of the faithful who live well? …. Thus their heart, where the intensity of compunction burns the fire and consumes the flesh, is called Altar of God". (Translated by me)

[447] M. G. BOYER, *The Liturgical Environment: What the Documents Say*, 48.

[448] M. G. BOYER, *The Liturgical Environment: What the Documents Say*, 48.

[449] L. EISENHOFER & J. LECHNER, *The Liturgy of the Roman Rite*, Herder and Herder, New York 1961, 126.

[450] M. J. BEHEN, «The Christian Altar», 422.

[451] R. GUARDINI, *Sacred Signs*, 36.

it is the hearthstone of the parochial family. Within its sacred precincts souls are given new birth in water and the Holy Spirit. The faithful are signed with the chrism of salvation for life's way of the cross. Upon its sacred fires the members of the household of the faith pour out their joys and sorrows, their labors, sufferings and anxieties, their achievements as well as their failures, and from its living coals the Bread of Life is broken for them to nourish their continued endeavors. To its parental warmth returns the prodigal son to confess his guilt and receive forgiveness. Around it the household gathers frequently to hear the word of God and to commune in family prayer. Its warmth enkindles the hearts of those who approach near enough to vow their life's ministration that these home-fires may be kept burning; and other hearts are welded, two into one, for the propagation of the household[452].

### 3.2.3. SOME GUIDELINES AND PROPOSALS FOR TODAY

A way of thinking about the Church, theologically and architecturally, is to begin with the Church's *raison d'être*, the holy Altar, and allow the building to grow out from there. It is the conviction of G. S. Duncan that if we design a material Altar which adequately portrays its meaning in our faith, and then allow the rest of the Church to reiterate, enframe and harmonize with the Altar, then we may be able to return the sense of the sacred to our modern Churches[453].

John Chrysostom emphasizes on the moral implications of sharing Eucharist. He found it strange that people provide vessels for the body and blood of Christ while neglecting the poor who are also the body of Christ[454]. Sri Lankan Roman Catholic theologian Tissa Balasuriya asks:

> Why is it that in spite of hundreds of thousands of Eucharistic celebrations, Christians continue as selfish as before? Why have the Christian peoples been the most cruel colonizers of human history? Why is the gap of income, wealth, knowledge and power growing in the world today and that in favor of the Christian peoples? Why is it that persons and people who proclaim Eucharistic love and sharing deprive the poor people of the world of food, capital, employment and even land?[455].

---

[452] E. MCDONALD, «The Consecration of the Altar», 308.
[453] G. S. DUNCAN, *The Church Building as a Sacred Place: Beauty, Transcendence, and the Eternal*, 20.
[454] D. POWER, *The Eucharistic Mystery: Revitalizing the Tradition*, 149.
[455] T. BALASURIYA, *The Eucharist and Human Liberation*, Orbis Books, New York 1979, xi-xii.

The identity of Christ at the table is incomplete if some are excluded, especially if the poor are left at the door. To be one in him we have to overcome all discriminations and all inequitable differences in our midst. At the table there is no difference between the wealthy and the poor, no difference except sinful one[456]. If we do not carry our concerns and those of the world when we come into church, there is no point in going. Likewise, if we do not carry our own commitments when we leave Church, then it was pointless to enter in the first place, since a Eucharist without willingness to commit oneself ethically, especially with regard to one's neighbor, is void. Without active commitments, worship is comfortable entertainment[457].

The author D. N. Power, narrates an incident in Bologna, Italy on a Sunday before the celebration of the Mass. The interior of the church was filled with the poor and the homeless and some parishioners were laying out tables of food the whole way down the nave. When inquired one of them asked in return, "How can we feed from the body of Christ unless we have fed the body of Christ?"[458].

When we take into account the use of the Altar in the parishes, some priests use it as a table of convenience. We give respect to other material objects such as national flags which are mere symbols. Then how much greater should our care for the Altar of sacrifice be?[459] Boyer states that the Altar is never used as a table of convenience or as a resting place for papers, notes, cruets, or anything else. Only corporal, purificator, missal, chalice, and bread are placed on the Altar[460]. Even GIRM insists this, saying, *"Etiam pecunia vel alia dona pro pauperibus vel pro ecclesia a fidelibus allata vel in ecclesia collecta accepta habentur; quapropter loco apto extra mensam eucharisticam collocantur"*[461]. As the General Instruction says other gifts are to be placed in a suitable place but not on the Altar. Furthermore, in order to continuously emphasize the dignity of the Altar, the rite of dedication of the Altar says in the instructions, "*In novis*

---

[456] D. N. POWER, «The Eucharistic Table: In communion with the Hungry», in *Worship* 83 (2009/5) 386-398, 386-387.
[457] C. GIRAUDO, «The Eucharist as Diakonia: From the service of cult to the service of Charity», in *Liturgy in the Postmodern World*, ed. K. Pecklers, Continuum, New York 2003, 102-132, 132.
[458] D. N. POWER, «The Eucharistic Table: In communion with the Hungry», 386.
[459] G. S. DUNCAN, *The Church Building as a Sacred Place: Beauty, Transcendence, and the Eternal*, 20.
[460] M. G. BOYER, *The Liturgical Environment: What the Documents Say*, 53.
[461] *Institutio Generalis Missalis Romani No. 117*, in *Missale Romanum Ex Decreto Sacrosancti Oecumenici Concilii Vaticani II, Instauratum auctoritate Pauli PP.VI promulgatum Ioannis Pauli PP. II cura recognitum*, 46.

*ecclesiis simulacra vel imgines Sanctorum supra Altare ne collocentur. Item ne deponantur super Altaris mensam Sanctorum reliquiae cum ad populi venerationem exhibentur*"[462].

When we focus on other elements like anointing, incensing, candles, Altar linen and flowers that are used, we have many guidelines and proposals for today. The Altar should be free-standing and clear of all non-essentials. Moreover, the cross and the candelabra should be on the Altar, or, according to the most ancient usage of the Church, near or around the Altar. If the priest faces the congregation, due conclusions should be drawn about removing or reducing visually obstructive objects. Microphones, if necessary, should be as visually inconspicuous as possible[463].

United States Conference of Catholic Bishops, in the document *Built of Living Stones number 92 & 93*, says:

> The candles or flowers should not obscure the view of the ritual action in the sanctuary, especially the action at the Altar. Candles for liturgical use should be made of a material that provides 'a living flame without being smoky or noxious'. To safeguard 'authenticity and the full symbolism of light', electric lights a substitute for candles are not permitted[464].

The same Bishops' Conference also adds instruction regarding the use of Altar candles. It says that candles are used to express both reverence and festivity. They should be consumed in giving its light. The candles may be placed on the Altar or, more appropriately, near or around it, so as not to distract from the Sacred Vessels or impede the participants' view of the liturgical action[465].

All candles used in the celebration of the Eucharist and in any other liturgical rites are to be made of Wax, because of their nature and imitation of candles should not be used in the liturgy. Nor should electrical bulbs be used in liturgical celebration. The use of other material either in substitutes for or in imitation of candles is not permitted

---

[462] *Ordo Dedicationis Ecclesiae et Altaris, Pontificale Romanum, Ex Decreto Sacrosancti Ecumenici Concili Vaticani II Instauratum Auctoritate Pauli PP. VI Promulgatum*, 51. tr. "In the new Churches statues and pictures of saints may not be placed above the Altar. Likewise, when relics of saints are exposed for veneration, they should not be placed on the table of the Altar". Quoted from *Dedication of a Church and an Altar*, 68.
[463] D. GODFREY, «The Place of Liturgical Worship», 93-94.
[464] UNITED STATES CONFERENCE OF CATHOLIC BISHOPS, *Built of Living Stones: Art, Architecture, and Worship*, 441-442.
[465] UNITED STATES CONFERENCE OF CATHOLIC BISHOPS, *Introduction to the Order of Mass: A Pastoral Resource of the Bishops' Committee on the Liturgy*, International Committee on English in the Liturgy, Washington 2003, 37-38.

in the liturgy. Nothing can satisfy the demand for the integrity in lights for liturgical use other than candles made of wax[466].

J. E. Mater, a parish priest in the city of Vienna, says, "The microphone should be inconspicuous. The candles and flowers are to be placed near the Altar without hiding the visibility of what takes place on the Altar. When no liturgy is being celebrated, the Altar is bare covered with Altar cloth. It awaits the sacred action"[467]. Stenta gives some guidelines for the floral decoration for the liturgy and its significance. During the Easter season and on feasts of our Lord only white flowers (yellow only by way of exception) can be a proper symbol. The Easter season, moreover, should be characterized by special floral decoration[468]. Kelmens states that on the feast of the saint or the martyr whose relic is placed in the Altar, the place may be adorned with flowers[469].

United States Conference of Catholic Bishops in their instruction warns that the top of the Altar itself holds only what is necessary for the celebration, for example, the Sacred Vessels and Roman Missal, and those things remain on the Altar only while needed. Decorative items like flowers may be placed near or around the Altar, but not on it[470]. Duncan also supports this point from his angle saying that the understanding of the meaning and holiness of the Altar will cause us to make it the most beautiful object possible[471]. Boyer instructs that the signs, symbols or slogans should not be embroidered or painted onto the Altar cloth. The Altar frontals filled with signs, decorated antependia, and the Altar covers displaying slogans definitely detract from the integrity of the Altar[472].

In insisting that the Altar is not a table of convenience, we can see the instructions given about keeping the gifts and even decorations not on the Altar. It is desirable that candles, cross, any flowers or other decoration in the area should not be so close to the Altar as to constitute impediments to anyone's approach or movement

---

[466] M. G. BOYER, *The Liturgical Environment: What the Documents Say*, 52.
[467] R. KELMENS, *The Meaning of the Sacramental Symbols: Answers to Todays Questions*, 148.
[468] N. STENTA, «Use of flowers in the Liturgy», 465.
[469] R. KELMENS, *The Meaning of the Sacramental Symbols: Answers to Todays Questions*, 149.
[470] UNITED STATES CONFERENCE OF CATHOLIC BISHOPS, *Introduction to the Order of Mass: A Pastoral Resource of the Bishops' Committee on the Liturgy*, 38.
[471] G. S. DUNCAN, *The Church Building as a Sacred Place: Beauty, Transcendence, and the Eternal*, 21.
[472] M. G. BOYER, *The Liturgical Environment: What the Documents Say*, 51.

around the common table. Decoration should never impede the approach to or encircling the Altar[473]. Built of living stone instructs in number 124, "decorations are intended to draw people to the true nature of the mystery being celebrated rather than being ends in themselves. Natural flowers, plants, wreaths and fabric hangings, and other seasonal objects can be arranged to enhance the primary liturgical points of focus. The Altar should remain clear and free-standing, not walled in by massive floral displays or the Christmas crib, and pathways in the narthex, nave, and sanctuary should remain clear"[474].

Since the audibility and visibility to all in the assembly are essential requirements, anything that hinders these should not be near the Altar. Therefore, bouquets of flowers placed in front of the Altar, nativity scenes erected in front of the Altar, banners pinned to the Altar, huge microphones set upon the Altar, or large bookstands resting on the Altar should be avoided. M. G. Boyer insists this, saying "large items either on front of or on the Altar create psychological blockades; these push the assembly from the common table while also pushing the table away from the assembly. An Altar with something in front of it tell people to stay away"[475].

## CONCLUSION TO THE THIRD CHAPTER

Gestures, veneration and symbolism have deep theological and liturgical meanings. As the image of rock is closely connected with Christ, it is encouraged to build Altar in one single stone, unbroken and without parts symbolizing the personal unity with Christ. Since thr Altar is Christ and the meeting place of God and man, incensing and kissing are done. The Altar is given respect and reverence only because of the Christological perspective.

Whenever the liturgy is celebrated, it is the sacrament of unity and the centre of the action of the Whole Church. Hence the Altar around which the community is gathered, is the centre of gravitational pull of the Church. Kissing is viewed from the aspect of bridal relationship between the Church and Christ. Altar linen is a symbol of

---

[473] M. G. BOYER, *The Liturgical Environment: What the Documents Say*, 53.
[474] UNITED STATES CONFERENCE OF CATHOLIC BISHOPS, *Built of Living Stones: Art, Architecture, and Worship*, 448.
[475] M. G. BOYER, *The Liturgical Environment: What the Documents Say*, 54.

members of the Church becoming one with Christ. The table calls the community to share their love through the meal in which Christ Himself is the heavenly food. Thus, these gestures, adornment and symbolism are ecclesiological. The Altar is the place where Christ's sacrifice is perpetuated. So, most of adornments bring out this sacrificial aspect. Candles, flowers, the Altar Cross and the Altar cloth are used to demonstrate this sacrificial aspect of the Altar.

I have tried to propose some of the ethical implications, some guidelines and some proposal for the daily lives and for the liturgical celebration from the gestures, symbolism and veneration with regard to the Altar. The Altar should be treated and venerated as though it is a living person, and not merely a living person, but as the Person of the Incarnate Son of God. As the liturgical gestures demand at least a minimum of preparation and care, the celebrants should pay much attention in them. Haste leaves no room at all for beauty and comprehension. Therefore, the gestures of the celebrants should be graceful. These gestures, symbolism and veneration are not merely cultic and outwardly. They call every Christian for a certain realization of the significance that they carry in them.

First of all, every Christian is a spiritual Altar. The Altar Candles and linen call the Christian to be faithful to the baptismal promises, to be a light of the world as his Master is and to be pure like the linen. The Communitarian aspects call him or her to overcome all discriminations and to reach out the needy because without active commitments, worship is comfortable entertainment. The Altar should never be taken lightly and used as a table of convenience. Only the essentials things can be kept near or around the Altar and not on it. On the top of the Altar, only what is necessary for the celebration can be placed. The adornment and decorations should not obscure the view of the ritual action in the sanctuary and especially the action on the Altar. The due reverence should be always shown to the Altar as it is Christ himself.

# GENERAL CONCLUSION

The Altar around which the community is gathered, is the centre of gravitational pull of the Church. As it symbolizes Christ Himself, it should be treated with great reverence. In this work, I have tried to explain how important the Altar is in the Christian worship by explaining in detail the biblical and historical background of the idea of Altar. The Altar is the place where heaven and earth meet and from where prayers ascend to God. Especially the Christian Altar is symbol of Christ, the body of Christ, the table of the Last Supper, the Cross of Calvary, the tomb of Christ's burial and Resurrection, the Altar in heaven, the ark of the New Covenant, the heavenly throne of God and every Christian. Such an important and glorious Altar is venerated in the Church with proper gestures and adornment.

These gestures and veneration should be performed with proper understanding. In this work, I have tried to bring out the theological and liturgical understanding of some of the gestures, adornment and symbolism with regard to the Altar. Actually all the liturgical actions, gestures and symbols are condensed with meaning and call for the understanding and realization in daily lives. There are some theological and liturgical understandings derived from the gestures, veneration and symbolism with regard to the Altar as I have tried to explain throughout this work, such as the sacrificial aspect that is in the candles, flowers, Cross and linen etc. As the liturgical gestures demand at least a minimum of preparation and care, the celebrants should pay much attention in them. Haste leaves no room at all for beauty and comprehension. These gestures, symbolism and veneration are not merely cultic and outwardly. They call every Christian for a certain realization of the significance that they carry in them.

In the liturgical implications, I have proposed some guidelines for the celebrants and participants of the liturgical celebration to be aware of what they celebrate and what is celebrated in the sanctuary. In the pastoral implications, the practical and daily lives of the people in relation to the Altar is discussed and I have tried to derive also some social and moral values like community spirit, sharing, equality and charity because without active commitments, worship is comfortable entertainment. This study calls for a right respect to the Altar and emphasizes that the Altar is not at all a convenient table to be taken lightly.

**Altar outdoor at St. Peter's Vatican at the canonization of Sts. John XXIII and John Paul II**

# BIBLIOGRAPHY

## 1. FONTS

### 1.1. BIBLICAL SOURCES

*The Holy Bible, The New Revised Standard Version*, Theological Publications of India, Bangalore 1993.

### 1.2. LITURGICAL SOURCES

*De Antiquis Ecclesiae Ritibus Libri: Ex variis insigniorum Ecclesiarum Pontificalibus, Sacramentariis, Missalibus, Breviariis, Ritualibus, seu Manualibus, Ordinariis seu Consuetudinariis, cum manuscriptis tum editis; ex diversis Conciliorum Decretis, Episcoporum Statutis, aliisque probatis Auctoribus permultis*, ed. E. Martene, Antuerpiae, Typis Joannis Baptistae de la Bry 1736.

*De Septem Ordinibus Ecclesiae*, in *Worship in the Early Church: An Anthology of Historical Sources Vol 3*, ed. & tr. L. J. Johnson, Liturgical Press, Minnesota 2009, 175-178.

*Documents on the Liturgy 1963-1979: Conciliar, Papal and Curial Texts*, ed., International Commission on English in the Liturgy, The Liturgical Press, Minnesota 1982.

*General Instruction of the Roman Missal: Liturgy Documentary Series 2*, tr. International Committee on English in the Liturgy, United states Conference of Catholic Bishops Publishing, Washington 2003.

*Institutio Generalis Missalis Romani,* in *Missale Romanum Ex Decreto Sacrosancti Oecumenici Concilii Vaticani II, Instauratum auctoritate Pauli PP.VI promulgatum Ioannis Pauli PP. II cura recognitum*, Typis Vaticanis, Citta del Vaticano ³2008, 17- 86.

INTERNATIONAL COMMISSION ON ENGLISH IN THE LITURGY, *Ceremonial of Bishops: Revised by Decree of the Second Vatican Ecumenical Council and Published by Authority of Pope John Paul II*, The Liturgical Press, Minnesota 1989.

*Liber Pontificalis*, in *Worship in the Early Church: An Anthology of Historical Sources Vol 4*, ed. & tr. L. J. Johnson, Liturgical Press, Minnesota 2009, 53-58.

*Liber Sacramentorum Romanæ Æclesiæ ordinis anni circuli* (Cod. Vat. Reg. lat. 316/Paris Bibl. Nat. 7193, 41/56) (*Sacramentarium Gelasianum*), ed. L. Eizenhofer-P. Siffrin-L. C. Mohlberg-(Rerum Ecclesiasticarum Documenta Series Maior, Fontes 4), Herder, Roma 1981.

*Memoriale Rituum: pro aliquibus praestantioribus sacris functionibus persolvendis in minoribus ecclesiis Benedicti XIII Pont. Max. jussu editum Benedicti Papae XV auctoritatae recognitum*, Typis Polyglottis Vaticanis, Romae 1950.

*Ordo Missae,* in *Missale Romanum Ex Decreto Sacrosancti Concilii Tridentini Restitutum Summorum Pontificum Cura Recognitum*, Editio Prima Iuxta Typicam, Sumptibus et Typis Mame, Romae 1962.

*Ordo Missae,* in *Missale Romanum Ex Decreto Sacrosancti Tridentini Restitutum Summorum Pontificum Cura Recognitum*, Editio Prima Iuxta Typicam, Sumptibus et Typis Mame, Romae-Turonibus-Parisiis 1969.

*Pontificale Romanum Summorum Pontificum Jussu Editum a Benedicto XIV. et Leone XIII. pont. max. recognitum et castigatum*, Pustet, Regensburg 1891.

*Praeparatio ad Missam*, in *Missale Romanum Ex Decreto Sacrosancti Oecumenici Concilii Vaticani II, Instauratum auctoritate Pauli PP.VI promulgatum, Ordo Missae*, Typis Polyglottis Vaticanis, Romae 1969.

*Rituale Romanum Ex Decreto Sanrosancti Oecumenici Concili Vaticani II Instauratum Auctoritate Ioannis Pauli II Promulgatum: De Benedictionibus,* Typis Polyglottis Vaticanis, Romae 1984.

*Rituale Romanum: Pauli V. Pontificis Maximi Jussu Editum et a Benedicto XIV actum et castigatum*, Typis S. Congregationis de Propaganda Fide, Romae 1847.

*Testamentum Domini Nostri Jesu Christi*, ed. & tr. I. E. Rahmani, Sumptibus Francisci Kirchheim, Mouguintiae 1899.

*Testamentum Domini Nostri Jesu Christi*, in *Worship in the Early Church: An Anthology of Historical Sources Vol 3*, ed. & tr. L. J. Johnson, Liturgical Press, Minnesota 2009, 305-336.

*The Didascalia Apostolorum in English (translated from the Syriac)*, tr. M. D. Gibson, Cambridge University press, London 1903.

*The Liturgy Documents Vol I&II*, ed., David Lysik, Liturgy Training Publications, Chicago 2004.

*The Roman Pontifical Revised by Decree of the Second Vatican Ecumenical Council and Published by Authority of Pope Paul VI. Dedication of a Church and an Altar*, tr. International Commission on English in the Liturgy, United States Catholic Conference, Inc., Washington 1989.

UNITED STATES CONFERENCE OF CATHOLIC BISHOPS, «Built of Living Stones (2000)», in *The Liturgy Documents Vol I*, ed., David Lysik, Liturgy Training Publications, Chicago 2004, 417-498.

--------------, *Introduction to the Order of Mass: A Pastoral Resource of the Bishops' Committee on the Liturgy*, International Committee on English in the Liturgy Inc., Washington 2003.

## 1.3. PATRISTIC SOURCES

AMBROSE, «Commentary on the Gospel of St Luke», in *Worship in the Early Church: An Anthology of Historical Sources Vol 2*, ed. & tr. L. J. Johnson, Liturgical Press, Minnesota 2009, 12-80.

-------------, «De Sacramentis (on the Sacraments)» , in *Worship in the Early Church: An Anthology of Historical Sources Vol 2*, ed. & tr. L. J. Johnson, Liturgical Press, Minnesota 2009, 40-69.

-------------, «De Corporum Inventione SS. Martyrum Protasi et Gervasi Sermones Duo :Epistola XXII, ad Marcellinam», in *Sancti Ambrosii Mediolanensis Episcopi, ecclesiae patris ac doctoris Opera Omnia ad mediolanenses codices pressius exacta*, ed. P. A. Ballerini, Typographia Sancti Josephi, Mediolani 1881, 157-164.

-------------, «De Sacramentis», in *Des Sacraments Des Mysteres*, ed. D.B. Botte, (Sources Chrétiennes 25), Paris 1949, 53-107.

AUGUSTINUS, «Sermo CCCX: In Natali Cypriani Martyris II», in *Collectio selecta SS. Ecclesiae Patrum complectens Exquitissima opera tum Dogmatica et Moralia, tum Apologetica et Oratoria: Sancti Aurelii Augustini Hipponensis Episcopi Operum Pars IV. Opera Oratoria*, ed. D. A. Caillau, Parent-Desbarres, Paris 1838, 101-103.

-------------, «Sermo CCCXVIII: De Martyre Stephano V», in *Collectio selecta SS. Ecclesiae Patrum complectens Exquitissima opera tum Dogmatica et Moralia, tum Apologetica et Oratoria: Sancti Aurelii Augustini Hipponensis Episcopi Operum Pars IV. Opera Oratoria,* ed. D. A. Caillau, Parent-Desbarres, Paris 1838, 142-146.

BALAI, «Hymn for the Dedication of a New Church», in *Worship in the Early Church: An Anthology of Historical Sources Vol 3*, ed. & tr. L. J. Johnson, Liturgical Press, Minnesota 2009, 287-288.

CAESARIUS, «Sermon 76: An admonition to kneel for prayer and to bow at the blessing», in *Worship in the Early Church: An Anthology of Historical Sources Vol 4*, ed. & tr. L. J. Johnson, Liturgical Press, Minnesota 2009, 106-107.

CANONS OF FATHER ATHANASIUS, in *Worship in the Early Church: An Anthology of Historical Sources Vol 2*, ed. & tr. L. J. Johnson, Liturgical Press, Minnesota 2009, 415-422.

CLEMENT D'ALEXANDRIE, *Les Stromates: Stomate VII*, ed. A. Boulluec (Sources Chrétiennes 428), Paris 1997.

-------------, «Carpets(Stomata)» in *Worship in the Early Church: An Anthology of Historical Sources Vol 1*, ed. & tr. L. J. Johnson, ed. & tr. L. J. Johnson, Liturgical Press, Minnesota 2009, 261-263.

CYRILLI ALEXANDRIAE, «De Adoratione in Spiritu et Veritate», in *Cyrilli Alexandriae Archiepiscopi Opera Quae Reperiri Potuerunt Omnia*, ed. J. P. Migne (PG 68), Thomus Primus, Paris 1864, 133-1126.

EPIPHANIUS, *Epiphanus II: Ancoratus und Panarion*, ed. K. Holl, (Die Griechischen Christlichen Schritsteller), Akademie-Verlag, Berlin 1922.

GREGORII MAGNI, *Homiliae in Hiezechielem*, ed. M. Adriaen, Città Nuova Editrice, Roma 1993.

GREGORY OF NAZIANUS, «Sermon on the day of Lights on which our Lord was baptized», in *Worship in the Early Church: An Anthology of Historical Sources Vol 2*, ed. & tr. L. J. Johnson, Liturgical Press, Minnesota 2009, 151-159.

JOHN CHRYSOSTOM, «Homilies on Second Letter to Corinthians», in *Worship in the Early Church: An Anthology of Historical Sources Vol 2*, ed. & tr. L. J. Johnson, Liturgical Press, Minnesota 2009, 171-211.

MAGNI FELICIS ENNODII, «Benedictio Cerei», in *Opera Omnia*, ed. G. Hartel, (Corpus Scriptorum Ecclesiasticorum 6), Vindobonae 1882, 415-422.

MINUCII FELICIS, «Octavius», in *Bibliotheca Sanctorum Patrum. Theologiae tironibus et universo clero accommadata* (Scriptores Latini, Series Tertia), ed. I. Vizzini, Ex Officina Typographica Forzani et Socii, Rome 1910, 1-90.

NARSAI OF NISIBUS, «Homilies», in *Worship in the Early Church: An Anthology of Historical Sources Vol 3*, ed. & tr. L. J. Johnson, Liturgical Press, Minnesota 2009, 288-305.

OPTAT DE MILÈVE, «Liber Sextus», in *Traité Contre Les Donatistes*, ed. M. Labrousse, (Sources Chrétiennes 413) Paris 1996, 160-191.

-------------, *The Work of St. Optatus: Against Donatists*, tr. O. R. V. Phillips, Longmans, Green & Co., London 1917.

ORIGÈNE, «Homilia II», in *Homélies sur Josué*, ed. A. Jaubert, (Sources Chrétiennes 71) Paris 1960, 116-123.

-------------, «Homily on Joshua», in *Worship in the Early Church: An Anthology of Historical Sources Vol 1*, ed. & tr. L. J. Johnson, Liturgical Press, Minnesota 2009, 246-257.

PAULINUS, «Letter to Severus», in *Worship in the Early Church: An Anthology of Historical Sources Vol 3*, ed. & tr. L. J. Johnson, Liturgical Press, Minnesota 2009, 104-109.

THEODORE OF MOPUSUETIA, «Homily on Eucharist», in *Worship in the Early Church: An Anthology of Historical Sources Vol 3*, ed. & tr. L. J. Johnson, Liturgical Press, Minnesota 2009, 246-275.

THOMAE AQUINATIS, «In Epistolam ad Hebraeos», in *Divi Thomae Aquinatis Doctoris Angelici Ordinis Praedicatorum. Opera VII-VIII*, Venetiis 1747, 407-584.

## 1.4. MAGISTERIAL DOCUMENTS

*Catechism of the Catholic Church*, Mambo Press, Gweru, 1992.

*Code of Canon Law Annotated*, ed. E. Caparros, Wilson & Lafleus Limitee, Montreal 1993.

CONCILIUM OECUMENICUM VATICANUM II, Constitutio de Sacra Liturgia *Sacrosanctum Concilium*, *AAS* 56 (1964) 97-138.

------------, Constitutio Dogmatica de Ecclesia *Lumen Gentium*, *AAS* 57 (1965) 5-71.

------------, Constitutio Pastoralis de Ecclesia in mundo huius temporis *Guadium et Spes 18*, *AAS 58* (1966) 1025-1118.

------------, Decretum de Activitate Missionali Ecclesiae *Ad Gentes 3*, *AAS* 58 (1966) 947-990.

------------, Decretum de Oecumenismo *Unitatis Redintegratio 15*, *AAS* 57 (1965) 90-112.

------------, Decretum de Presbyterorum Ministerio et Vita *Presbyterorum Ordinis*, *AAS 58* (1966) 991-1024.

CONSILIUM, «*Des gestes qui revelent,* on gentures in the Liturgy (January 1968)», in *Documents on the Liturgy 1963 – 1979, Conciliar, Papal, and Curial Texts*, The Liturgical Press, Minnesota 1982, 146-147.

------------, «Letter *Le renouveau liturgique* of Cardinal G. Lercaro to presidents of the conference of bishops, on furthering liturgical reform (30 June 1965)», in *Documents on the Liturgy 1963 – 1979, Conciliar, Papal, and Curial Texts*, The Liturgical Press, Minnesota 1982, 117-122.

------------, «Letter *Le renouveau liturgique* of Cardinal G. Lercaro to presidents of the conference of bishops, on furthering liturgical reform (30 June 1965)» in *Documents on the Liturgy 1963 – 1979, Conciliar, Papal, and Curial Texts*, The Liturgical Press, Minnesota 1982, 117-122.

JOHN PAUL II, *Vicesimus Quintus Annus, Quinto iam lustro expleto conciliari ab promulgata de Sacra Liturgia Constitutione Sacrosanctum Concilium*, *AAS 81* (1989) 897-918.

PIUS XII, «Litterae encyclicae *Mediator Dei et hominum* (20 novembris 1947)», in *AAS* 39 (1947) 521-595.

SACRA CONGREGATIO RITUUM, «Ad Instructionem 101», *Notitiae 2* (1966) 21-22.

------------, *Instructio altera: Tres abhinc annos*, ad exsecutionem constitutionis de sacra liturgia recte ordinandam, *AAS 59* (1967) 442-448.

------------, *Instructio: ad exsecutionem constitutionis de sacra liturgia recte ordinandam*, *AAS 56* (1967) 877-900.

SC RITES (Consilium), «Instruction (first) *Inter Oecumenici,* on the orderly carrying out of the Constitution on the Liturgy, 26 September 1964», in *Documents on the Liturgy 1963 – 1979, Conciliar, Papal, and Curial Texts*, The Liturgical Press, Minnesota 1982, 88-110.

------------, «Instruction (second) *Tres abhinc annos,* on the orderly carrying out of the Constitution on the Liturgy, 4 May 1967», in *Documents on the Liturgy 1963 – 1979, Conciliar, Papal, and Curial Texts*, The Liturgical Press, Minnesota 1982, 135-140.

## 2. STUDIES

### 2.1. BOOKS

*A Manual of the Ceremonies of Low Mass*, ed. L. Kuenzel, Frederick Pustet Co., New York 1930.

ANSON P. F., *Churches their plan and Furnishing*, edd. T. F. Croft & H. A. Reinhold, The Bruce Publishing Company, Milwaukee 1948.

BALASURIYA T., *The Eucharist and Human Liberation*, Orbis Books, New York 1979.

BOUYER L., *Liturgy and Architecture*, University of Notre Dame Press, Indiana 1967.

------------, *The Liturgy Revived*, Darton Longman & Todd, London 1965.

BOYER M. G., *The Liturgical Environment: What the Documents Say*, The Liturgical Press, Collegeville 1990.

BRADLEY J. P., *The Catholic Layman's Library Vol 3*, Goodwill Publishers Inc, North Carolina 1970.

BRIDGET T., *A History of the Holy Eucharist in Great Britain*, C. Kegan Paul & Co, London 1881.

CHENGALIKAVIL L., *The Mystery of Christ and the Church in the Dedication of a Church*, Pontificium Athenaeum Anselmianum, Rome 1984.

DIX G., *Shape of the Liturgy*, Dacre Press, Westminster 1945.

EISENHOFER L. & LECHNER J., *The Liturgy of the Roman Rite*, Herder and Herder, New York 1961.

FERNANDES C. C., *The Eucharist: the Paschal Mystery and the New Covenant, Theological Publications in India*, Bangalore 1985.

FERRARO G., *Cristo è l'altare: Liturgia di dedicatione della chiesa e dell'altare*, Edizioni OCD, Roma 2004.

FORTESCUE A. & O'CONNELL J. B., *The Ceremonies of the Roman Rite Described*, Burns & Oates Ltd., London 1962.

GUARDINI R., *Sacred Signs*, tr. G. Branham, Pio Decimo Press, Missouri 1956

-------------, *The Church and the Catholic and the Spirit of Liturgy*, tr. A. Lane, Sheed & ward, New York 1940.

GUZIE T., *Jesus and the Eucharist*, Gracewing, Leominster 1995

HEGER P., *The Three biblical Altars*, Werner Hildebrand, Berlin 1999.

HOVDA R. W., *Strong, Loving and Wise : Presiding in Liturgy*, The Liturgical Press, Collegeville 1976.

IGNAZIO M.C., *The Dedication of a Church and al Altar: A Theological Commentary*, United States Catholic Conference, Washington 1980.

JUNGMANN J., *The Early Liturgy: To the Time of Gregory the Great*, Tr. Brunner Francis, University of Notre Dame Press, Indiana 1959.

------------, *The Mass of the Roman Rite: Its Origin and Development Vol I&II*, Tr. Francis A. Brunner, Christian Classic Inc., Maryland 1986.

KELMENS R., *The Meaning of the Sacramental Symbols: Answers to Today's Questions*, The Liturgical Press, Minnesota 1990.

KEVIN W. I., *Models of the Eucharist*, Paulist Press, New York 2005.

KIECKHEFER R., *Theology in Stone: Church Architecture from Byzantium to Berkeley*, Oxford University Press, New York 2004.

LANG J. P., *Dictionary of the Liturgy*, Catholic Book Publishing Corp., New York 1989.

MAZZA E., *The Celebration of the Eucharist: Origin of the Rite and Development of its Interpretation*, tr. M. J. O'Connell, The Liturgical Press, Minnesota 1999.

NICHOLAS M., *Altars according to the Code of Canon Law*, The Catholic University of America, Washington 1927.

O'CONNELL J. B., *Church Building and Furnishing*, Burns & Oates, London 1955.

O'CONNELL L. J., *The Book of ceremonies*, The Bruce Publishing company, Wisconsin 1943

PECKLERS K. F., *Worship: A New Century Theology*, Continuum, London 2003.

PODHRADSKY G., *New Dictionary of the Liturgy*, ed. L. Sheppard, Geoffrey Chapman, London 1967.

POWER D., *The Eucharistic Mystery: Revitalizing the Tradition*, Crossroads, New York 1994.

RATZINGER J., *The Spirit of the Liturgy*, tr. John Saward, Ignatius Press, San Francisco 2000.

SALAVILLE S., *An Introduction to the Study of Eastern Liturgies*, Sands & Co, London 1938.

UNDERHILL E., *Worship*, Harper & Brothers Publishers, New York 1937.

VALENZIANO, *L'anello della sposa: Mistagogia Eucaristica I. Modulazione circolare del Rito*, Centro Liturgico Vincenziano, Roma 2005.

## 2.2. ARTICLES

BATCHELDER D. B., «Holy God, Dangerous Liturgy: Preparing the Assembly for Transforming Encounter», in *Worship 79* (2005/4) 290-303.

BEHEN M.J., «The Christian Altar», in *Worship 26* (1952) 422-428.

BOWMAN T.B., «2 Corinthians 2:14-16a: Christ's incense», in *Restoration Quarterly 29* (1987/2) 65-69.

BUSSARD, P. C., «Altar Alteration», in *Orate Fratres 13* (1938) 66-71.

CARNEIRO A. R., «Realizzazioni di Altari in Francia e in Belgio», in *L'altare*, ed., G. Boselli, Edizioni Qiqajon, Magnano 2003, 99-112.

CLERCK P. D., «Il Significato dell'Altare nei Rituali della Dedicazione», in *L'altare*, ed. G. Boselli, Edizioni Qiqajon, Magnano 2003, 39-55.

CORNELIS H., «On the function of the holy incense (Exodus 30:34-8) and the sacred anointing oil (Exodus 30:22-33) », in *Vetus Testamentum 42* (1992/4) 458-465.

DEBUYST F., «L'altare: Opera d'arte o Mistero di Presenza?», in *L'altare*, ed. G. Boselli, Edizioni Qiqajon, Magnano 2003, 27-38.

DOHMEN C., «Mizbeah», in *The Theological Dictionary of the Old Testament Vol VIII*, ed. Johannes Botterweek, William B Eermans Publishing Company, Cambridge 1997, 209-225.

EDSMAN C., «Altar», in *The Encyclopedia of Religion Vol I*, ed. Eliade Mircea, Macmillan Publishing Company, New York 1987, 222-226.

FERRARO G., «Cristo è l'Altare : Considerazioni sulla Tematica Cristologica nell 'Ordo Dedicationis Ecclesiae et Altaris'», in *Notitiae 33* (1997) 72-86.

----------, «Il Mistero di Cristo nella liturgia della dedicazione», in *La Civilta Cattolica 133* (1986/3) 239-251.

GERHARDS A., «Teologia dell'Altare», in *L'altare*, ed., G. Boselli, Edizioni Qiqajon, Magnano 2003, 213-232.

GIRAUDO C., «The Eucharist as Diakonia: From the service of cult to the service of Charity», in *Liturgy in the Postmodern World*, ed. K. Pecklers, Continuum, New York 2003, 102-132.

GODFREY D., «Altar and Tabernacle», in *Worship 40* (1966/8) 490-509.

----------, «The Place of Liturgical Worship», in *The Church and the Liturgy Vol 2*, ed., Johannes Wagner, Paulist Press, New Jersey 1964, 67-107.

GRAY D., «Hands and Hocus-Pocus : The Manual Acts in the Eucharistic Prayer», in *Worship 69* (1995/4) 306-313.

GRAY L., «Altar», in *Encyclopedia of Religion and Ethics Vol I*, ed. James Hastings, T & T Clark, New York 1967, 333-354.

GUARDINI R., «La funzione della sensibilità nella conoscenza religiosa», in *Scritti filosofici vol II*, Fabbri, Milano 1964, 135-190.

GWINN R., «Altar», in *The New Encyclopedia Britannica Vol I (Micropedia)*, ed. P. W. Goetz, Encyclopedia Britannica Inc, Chicago 1986, 298.

HEID S., «The Early Christian Altar – Lessons for Today», in *Sacred Liturgy: The Source and Summit of the Life and Mission of the Church*, ed. A. Reid, Ignatius Press, San Francisco 2014, 87-114.

HIEBERT T., «Altars of Stone and Bronze: Two Biblical Views of Technology», in *Mission Studies 15* (1998/2) 75-84.

HUCK G. D., «Symbolism of Flowers», in *The New Catholic Encyclopedia of Religion Vol 5*, ed. W. J. McDonald, McGraw-Hill Book Company, New York 1967, 981-982.

JONES P. H., «We are How we Worship : Corporate Worship as a Matrix for Christian Identity Formation», in *Worship 69* (1995/4) 346-360.

JUNGMANN J., «The New Altar», in *Liturgical Arts 37* (1969/2) 36-39.

KEARNEY P. J., «Altar in the Bible», in *New Catholic Encyclopedia Vol I*, ed. W. J. Mc Donald, McGraw-Hill Book Company, New York 1967, 344-346.

LILLEY., «The altar in Joshua and Judges», in *Tynadale House Bulletin* (1960) 32-33.

MAGGIANI S., «Il symbolo della Croce nello Spazio Liturgico», in *Rivista Liturgica 101* (2014/1) 111-129.

-------------, «The Language of Liturgy», in *Liturgical Science* II, ed. A. J, Chupungco, A Pueblo Book, Minnesota 227-255.

MAZZA E., «Tavola e Altare: Due Modi non Alternativi per Designare un Oggetto Liturgico», in *L'altare*, ed. G. Boselli, Edizioni Qiqajon, Magnano 2003, 55-81.

MCDONALD E., «The Consecration of the Altar», in *Orate Fratres 6* (1932/7) 308-312.

-------------, «The Consecration of the Altar», in *Orate Fratres 6* (1932/8) 359-365.

-------------, «The Consecration of the Altar», in *Orate Fratres 6* (1932/9) 410-415.

MCKENNA J. H., «Eucharist and Sacrifice : an Overview», in *Worship 76* (2002/5) 386-402.

MILLER J. H., «Altar facing the people: fact or fable?», in *Worship 33* (1959/2) 83-91.

NAPIER C., «The Altar in the Contemporary Church», in *The Clergy Review 57* (1972/8) 624-632.

POWER D. N., «The Eucharistic Table: In communion with the Hungry», in *Worship 83* (2009/5) 386-398.

RICHTER K., «Comunita, Spazio Liturgico e Altare», in *L'altare*, ed., G. Boselli, Edizioni Qiqajon, Magnano 2003, 181-200.

ROBINSON B., «The Christ Church Cathedral Altar Cloth Controversy : Upanishadic Text and Eucharistic Context», in *Colloquium 39* (2007/1) 58-78.

SISTER J., «The altar is Christ», in *Orate Fratres* 11 (1937/12) 549-554.

STENTA N., «Use of flowers in the Liturgy», in *Orate Fratres 4* (1930/11) 462-469.

WIENER H. M., «Altar», in *The International Standard Bible Encyclopedia Vol I*, ed. G. F. Bromiley, William B. Eerdmans Publishing Company, Michigan 1979, 100-104.

WILBRICHT S. S., «An Ecclesiological Interpretation of the Rite of Church Dedication», in *Worship 80* (2006/4) 326-346.